Are You

In an impassioned defence of the importance of our own thoughts, feelings and experiences, the renowned philosopher Mary Midgley shows that there's much more to our selves than a jumble of brain cells. Exploring the remarkable gap that has opened up between our understanding of our sense of self and today's science, Midgley argues powerfully and persuasively that the rich variety of our imaginative life cannot be contained in the narrow bounds of a highly puritanical materialism that simply equates brain and self.

Engaging with the work of prominent thinkers, Midgley investigates the source of our current attitudes to the self and reveals how ideas, traditions and myths have been twisted to fit in, seemingly naturally, with science's current preoccupation with the physical and material. Midgley shows that the subjective sources of thought – our own experiences – are every bit as necessary in helping to explain the world as the objective ones such as brain cells.

Are You an Illusion? offers a salutary analysis of science's claim to have done away with the self and a characteristic injection of common sense from one of our most respected philosophers into a debate increasingly in need of it.

This Routledge Classics edition includes a new Foreword by Stephen Cave.

Mary Midgley (1919–2018) was one of the leading moral philosophers of her generation and has been described by *The Guardian* as "the foremost scourge of scientific pretension in this country". Many of her books are available in Routledge Classics, including *Beast and Man*, *Wickedness* and *The Myths We Live By*.

"Routledge Classics is more than just a collection of texts... it embodies and circulates challenging ideas and keeps vital debates current and alive."

— *Hilary Mantel*

The Routledge Classics series contains the very best of Routledge's publishing over the past century or so, books that have, by popular consent, become established as classics in their field. Drawing on a fantastic heritage of innovative writing published by Routledge and its associated imprints, this series makes available in attractive, affordable form some of the most important works of modern times.

For a complete list of titles visit:
https://www.routledge.com/Routledge-Classics/book-series/SE0585

Mary
Midgley

Are You an Illusion?

With a new Foreword by Stephen Cave

 London and New York

Cover image: Lisa Vlasenko / Getty Images

First published in Routledge Classics 2023
by Routledge
4 Park Square, Milton Park, Abingdon, Oxon OX14 4RN

and by Routledge
605 Third Avenue, New York, NY 10158

Routledge is an imprint of the Taylor & Francis Group, an informa business

First published in 2014 by Acumen

British Library Cataloguing-in-Publication Data
A catalogue record for this book is available from the British Library

ISBN: 978-1-032-53371-1 (hbk)
ISBN: 978-1-032-53368-1 (pbk)
ISBN: 978-1-003-41171-0 (ebk)

DOI: 10.4324/9781003411710

Typeset in Joanna
by codeMantra

For Heather

CONTENTS

Foreword to the Routledge Classics Edition

I first met Mary Midgley in June 2012, two years before this book was first published. We were backstage at an event in Hay-on-Wye, a village on the English–Welsh border which is small and sleepy except in festival season, when thousands of book-lovers arrive to meet their favourite authors. She was 92 and swept in wearing her trademark wide-brimmed black hat. Her talk was a luminous account of the metaphors that shape scientific thinking, drawing widely on her oeuvre, including immensely original and influential works such as *Science and Poetry* (Routledge, 2001), *The Myths We Live By* (Routledge, 2003) and *The Solitary Self: Darwin and the Selfish Gene* (Routledge, 2010). The audience was captivated, as was I.

The ethicist Philippa Foot described the Midgley she had known in the 1930s at Somerville College, Oxford, as "a very grand figure indeed" (Brown, 2001). When I met her seven decades later, her grandeur was undiminished. Her influence and renown, on the other hand, had grown exponentially. Famously, she did not even begin to publish until she was in her 50s: her first book, *Beast and Man: The Roots of Human Nature*, was published in 1978 when she was 59. Prior to that, she worked in the civil service, as a high school teacher and as a lecturer in philosophy at Reading then Newcastle universities, while also taking time out to raise three sons. But the reason she herself gave for not writing until later in life was "because I didn't know what I thought before then" (Brown, 2001).

This coy statement hints at two of the reasons why Midgley's voice has been so clear and important ever since. First – contrary to the view in certain corners of academia that only youthful minds can produce cutting-edge work – her age and experience underpinned some of her keenest insights. Her specialty was seeing intellectual movements for the fashions they are, each with its particular origins, assumptions and limitations. It helps then that she experienced first-hand the rise and fall of many movements – such as logical positivism and behaviourism in the academy, not to mention the extremes of Marxism and fascism through the tumultuous mid-twentieth century.

Second, Midgley's modest claim that she did not know what she thought – and therefore did not publish – until her 50s is evidence of the high standards she had for what counted as a thought worth having. She was dismissive of "a particular style of philosophising that results from encouraging a lot of clever young men to compete in winning arguments" (Midgley 2013). This turned philosophy, she thought, into a kind of petty game-playing, of no interest to the wider world – or to her. The real business of philosophy, she believed, is the "big, difficult issues" (this book, p.17) – those that cross academic disciplines, and indeed underpin them, and connect those disciplines with the real meanings and mysteries of being human. It is just such big, difficult issues that she confronts in this book.

Indeed, the issue at the core of this book could hardly be bigger or more central to what it means to be human: it is whether you (or I or anyone else) really exist. The book is an elegant, richly informed rebuttal of the fashionable idea that, as Francis Crick put it: "your memories and your ambitions, your sense of personal identity and your free-will, are in fact no more than the behaviour of a vast assembly of nerve-cells and their attendant molecules" (quoted on p.5 of this book). Most valuably, Midgley not only shows that this claim to non-existence, this metaphysical suicide or self-icide, makes no sense, but also why so many eminent thinkers have been convinced that it does.

On one telling, this story begins with the French philosopher René Descartes being overly impressed by the ingenious clockwork automata on display in seventeenth-century Paris. The sophistication of these wondrous items convinced Descartes that living things too might be nothing but complex machines – all except humans, that is, who were made in the image of God and consequently possessed something further: a spiritual stuff that made us conscious, feeling beings. Of course, Descartes' work reflected the spirit of the times, or it would not have shaped the world as it did. Among other things, it created a space for the scientific investigation of the material world that still preserved a realm for the spiritual. At the time, this was an important accommodation with still-powerful religious authorities. But it also prepared the way for today's self-icide.

Dualism, as Midgley makes clear, effectively strips the material world of all mentality. It therefore leaves anyone who wishes to believe they are a conscious self needing also to believe in some immaterial soul-stuff. For someone who has given up religion and is unimpressed by evidence of the supernatural, this is an uncomfortable place to be. From this starting point, the "scientific" approach appears to be to dismiss mentality, consciousness and selves altogether.

But, as Midgely argues so convincingly, this is the wrong starting point. We are not advancing beyond the error of dualism by dismissing the mind side of the duality while still accepting the idea of matter as inherently and irredeemably mindless. Rather, to move beyond the wrong-headed divide introduced by dualism is to embrace the idea that matter itself can – and does – give rise to mindful creatures like ourselves, capable of self-awareness and art, understanding and feeling.

Contrary to Crick and others, in showing that the mind and the self are products of the brain and body, science has not shown that the mind and self therefore do not exist. This claim is not science but scientism – the dogmatic view that only science (and usually only one version of science, based on particular contingent assumptions, using a particular set of instruments) can provide us with knowledge of the world and the human condition.

As Midgley makes clear throughout this book, while eminent thinkers might profess such scientistic creeds, even they themselves do not live by them – they do not turn to brainscans or talk about neurons when seeking to explain the social world. They read historical accounts of the beliefs and ambitions of politicians past if they want to understand world events, or employ straightforward psychological accounts of their spouses' beliefs and ambitions in order to decide what to do at the weekend. Seeing humans as assemblies of nerve cells, it turns out, is only good for certain specific purposes.

For Midgley, the notion that science – or the science of the day – provides a uniquely true account of the world is a myth. By this she means not merely that it is untrue, but that it is a particular imaginative vision, supported by its own narrative and imagery and laden with particular interests and values. This rehabilitation of the idea of the myth is one of her greatest contributions: since the Enlightenment, many in the West have been tempted to see other peoples as guided by myths while they, by contrast, are the first people in history to be wholly clear-sighted and rational. Throughout her work, Midgley shows this presumption to be arrogant folly, and teaches us how to see the myths we ourselves live by (to borrow the title of one of her books).

Extending this idea, we can see how this book situates the myth of scientism and the myth of the illusory self within a broader mythology: a loose framework of interlocking stories with a long history. She traces it back to Pythagoreanism and Platonism, and those philosophies' reverence for the perceived purity of mathematics and disdain or even denial of our messy animality. These myths survived in certain strands of Christianity and were embraced by the founding figures of the scientific method. They persisted in recent centuries in the elevation of maths and physics as the purest forms of knowledge, and in the denigration of "untamed" nature. As Midgley skilfully shows in this book and others, this denigration of nature has also been extended to women and non-human animals, legitimating sexism and patriarchy, vivisection and factory farming, and the despoliation of the planet.

It is now over a century since Mary Midgley was born, and the intellectual causes for which she fought have seen many victories: feminism (not a term with which she identified, but a cause she advanced nonetheless) has become increasingly mainstream; the scientific community now widely accepts that non-human animals have thoughts and feelings; and the idea that we are profoundly interconnected with a complex biosphere has inspired activist and academic movements alike. But these wars are far from won. The myths that legitimate folly and injustice persist. We still need Mary Midgley's extraordinary ability to expose them for what they are.

Stephen Cave, April 2023

REFERENCES

Brown, Andrew. 2001. Mary, Mary, quite contrary. *The Guardian*.

Midgley, Mary. 1978. *Beast and Man: The Roots of Human Nature*. Routledge.

Midgley, Mary. 2001. *Science And Poetry*. Routledge.

Midgley, Mary. 2003. *The Myths We Live By*. Routledge.

Midgley, Mary. 2005. *The Owl of Minerva: A Memoir*. Routledge.

Midgley, Mary. 2010. *The Solitary Self: Darwin and the Selfish Gene*. Routledge.

Midgley, Mary. 2013. The golden age of female philosophy. *The Guardian*.

PREFACE

The only parts of this little book that have been printed before are some discussions drawn from my article "Why the Idea Of Purpose Won't go Away", which appeared in *Philosophy* (October 2011), 545–63. These are developed in Chapters 5–7 here.

The rest of the book simply flows from my increasing exasperation at the current tendency of many well-qualified scholars to claim, apparently in the name of science, that they believe themselves, and indeed their readers, not to exist, selves having apparently been replaced by arrangements of brain cells.

I think I understand why people sign up for this surprising story. They easily come to see it as a necessary pillar of their faith in science: a vindication of the material world; a crucial prop for the certainty that, in today's widespread disorder, we so badly need. It seems, too, to provide a stern, manly substitute for the more self-indulgent notion that our own thoughts and feelings actually matter.

But I don't think this suicidal device can give us our scientific certainty. The claim to non-existence does not really make sense in itself, nor does the reasoning that is used to support it. And that claim does not actually flow from science. It comes from an old dualistic philosophical tradition that now has no real authority. This damaged framework can't give any real support to science today. It can only injure its reputation.

In working out these thoughts I have had a great deal of help from colleagues and friends who share my scepticism about this quick way out of our troubles. Notably useful suggestions have come from Iain McGilchrist, Steven Rose, Andrew Brown, Ian Ground, Willie Charlton and (as always) from my three sons, especially David. Most of these people have been no more surprised than I am to see the idea of the self suddenly disappearing like this up the chimney. Anyone watching its fate during the past fifty years has seen this whole idea growing progressively thinner, vanishing repeatedly behind various machines, being fragmented to suit the terms of a dozen disciplines and (most crucially) being deliberately ignored by professional philosophers who were trying to make their study as impersonal, technical and generally science-like as possible. Abolishing the self is just the natural terminus of that process. But we still badly need to understand the process itself, and to discover what kind of world it leaves for those of us who (somewhat surprisingly) survive its impact. That is what I have tried to look into in this book.

It does seem possible that this whole ill-fated campaign – this march away from direct experience – which received the name "modern" a hundred years ago, may already be beginning to lose ground somewhat in our culture. If so, I can only hope that, in however slight a degree, I may be able to help it on its way.

INTRODUCTION
ARE WE LOSING OURSELVES?

This book is about a remarkable gap that has opened up between common sense and today's scientific orthodoxy, centrally about the idea that science has shown that our inner selves are mere illusions. In an important sense (it seems) we do not exist.

When something supposedly scientific clashes with common sense like this, we naturally tend to assume that common sense must be wrong. We know, for instance, that common sense *was* wrong when it used to suppose that the earth was flat or that the stars were all points on a continuous ceiling. We approve of the people who corrected these ideas. We think the new facts carried their own authority and that, in those cases, science did indeed need to trump common sense.

But it would be very odd – wouldn't it? – to suppose that it ought to do so always, or even often. For instance, when

DOI: 10.4324/9781003411710-1

science tells us that the tables we believe to be solid are largely composed of empty space we don't have to abandon our previous views and stop putting our cups down on them. Common sense can easily accommodate two different ways of thinking about tables. It has got used to fitting the microscopic view of things into the macroscopic one. It has developed a background system by which it can see roughly how to relate them. In this way, yesterday's science either gets fitted into today's common sense or – if it proves to be wrong – simply gets forgotten. Today, gravity is a matter of common sense and no one talks about epicycles.

Common sense, in fact, can grow and indeed it is always growing. It is not a fixed, unchanging formula that is always at odds with science, as Lewis Wolpert suggested in his book *The Unnatural Nature of Science* (1992). "I would almost contend", Wolpert wrote "that if something fits in with common-sense it can't be science ... The way in which the universe works is not the way in which common-sense works; the two are not congruent" (1992: 11).

But the way in which the universe works isn't confined to the things that the sciences tell us about it. That universe has hugely many aspects. It includes ourselves and our direct perceptions. It also includes the views of life that have been built up through aeons of human experience. That history has gone into building the background of today's common sense, which is not a fixed formula, comparable to a particular science, but is something more like a great stretch of mental countryside full of different kinds of vegetation – life forms that keep developing to suit what is going on around them.

Science too is itself, of course, not (as Wolpert suggests) a static, independent organism. It is simply one of the enterprising plants that have taken root in that countryside and have spread to transform great parts of the human landscape. Like other intellectual disciplines – history, poetry, music, mathematics and the rest – science has grown out of the pre-existing social soil and is wholly dependent on it. Like them, it is a subculture.

It has to start from the data that humans normally perceive and to develop those data in ways that suit the human mind. If, therefore, people claim that science has discovered something that is contrary to direct human perceptions and to those basic human thought patterns – as is happening now about the Self – then those people have to be mistaken. This is not a disagreement about an external fact such as the earth's shape. It is about what makes sense at all in a human context.

Thus the point from which we started – that common sense must sometimes give way to scientific facts – needs a slight complication. New suggestions must be accepted, but only if they can be understood in ways that fit with what is essential in the general human vision. If that can't be done we should suspect there is something wrong. And claims do not, of course, become scientific merely because certain scientists recite them. Scientists can, after all, make mistakes like anyone else. And science is unfortunately not composed of ready-made facts. People who formulate those facts have to use *assumptions*: patterns of expectation, within which they select, arrange, shape and classify their data, since these can at first seem very confused.

PRESUPPOSITION TROUBLE

We usually take these patterns of expectation for granted because they lie so deep in our thought, so far from consciousness that it can be quite hard even to detect them. Digging them out and articulating them is the business of philosophy, which often does make them a bit more intelligible. But even when they have been dug out they often still remain mysterious and certainly they are not necessarily reliable. They are not eternal verities. They are partly formed by the surrounding culture, which changes constantly. They can change with it, rather as currents deep below the earth change with shifts in the tectonic plates around them.

Indeed, they do change like this all the time. These changes have perhaps been obscured by calling them "paradigms". That name may suggest something ponderous and lasting, an arrangement that is with us for a century or so. But, as the inhabitants of Greece and Turkey know, tectonic plates are a lot more lively than that, and so are cultural climates. What changes is not just a particular set of beliefs but an attitude, a way of responding to the world, a way that is always being formed by a whole crowd of influences and affects everything we do.

These attitudes are expressed in changing *myths*, which are not lies but imaginative visions, pictures that show in graphic form how we see the world around us. (I have explained my understanding of this useful word before in *The Myths We Live By* [2003], so I shan't do so here.) The myth to which I especially want to draw attention now is the one that credits science – physical science – with a rather odd central role in our lives.

This myth pictures our world as a vast mass of physical objects that are being observed from a great distance by an anonymous observer through a huge array of telescopes. It is not by chance that this observer himself is anonymous, and indeed invisible, because he is not a proper object at all. Like the telescopes, he is simply a part of the apparatus that is needed to observe and record this endless range of facts. The whole process of observing and recording is called "Science" and is seen as constituting a central purpose of human life. As Steven Weinberg put it, "the effort to understand the universe is one of the very few things that lifts human life a little above the level of farce, and gives it some of the grace of tragedy" (1977: 155). In short, it is one of the most valuable things in human life.

What are the others? Weinberg does not say. Similarly, when he found it hard to persuade his fellow Americans to stump up for a Superconducting Supercollider that would outclass Europe's Large Hadron Collider, he pleaded that such constructions ought to be built because they are "the cathedrals of our age". We ought not (he said) to fall behind our medieval ancestors in providing them.

He did not explain what congregation wants these cathedrals or what deity they exist to honour. And the trouble here is not just that few people understand this sort of physics at all. It is that – if the story we shall be examining about the unreality of our own sensibilities is true – even those few people cannot want them because, essentially, they cannot really want anything. As Francis Crick puts it: "You, your joys and sorrows, your memories and your ambitions, your sense of personal identity and your free-will, are in fact no more than the behaviour of a vast assembly of nerve-cells and their attendant molecules" (Crick 1994: 3). There is nobody, then, who actually needs these shrines or the worship performed in them. Yet the profoundly reverent demand for it still persists.

WHAT IS SCIENTISM?

This picture is the worldview that is sometimes called scientism, a credo that, as we shall see, has very interesting metaphysical and religious roots and that is quite powerful today. It does not actually consist in an excessive reverence for science. Indeed, perhaps we can never feel too much reverence for science, or for any branch of knowledge. Knowledge is indeed wonderful and should be revered. Scientism's mistake does not lie in over-praising one form of it, but in cutting that form off from the rest of thought, in treating it as a victor who has put all the rest out of business.

Scientism exalts the *idea* of science on its own, causing people to become fixated on the assumptions that seemed scientific to them during their formative years. This prevents them from seeing contrary facts, however glaring they may be, that have been noticed more lately. The prime example of this at present is people's refusal – widespread, especially in the USA – to admit the reality of danger from climate change. This refusal persists staunchly in the teeth of today's well-qualified scientific opinion in a way that shows how strong its ideological roots are. It is, of course, also backed by people's natural laziness and by the fuel industries, which don't want a change. But there is more to this refusal than that. The ideology that makes it so hard for us to understand that anything is wrong here – the creed that tells us the human race is invulnerable – is a set of old and deep assumptions that are still seen as scientific, but which lie so deep in our thought that we do not easily recognize them. These assumptions generate bad science and we shall try to explore them in this book.

Let us start by considering why the attempt to glorify science on its own cannot work. This is because human thought operates as a whole. It is an ecosphere, a vast and complex landscape, including, but not confined to, common sense. Science itself is, of course, not a single compartment but a large, thickly wooded area comprising many sciences, an area that merges into those around it. Those sciences vary from physics to anthropology and all of them are shot through with problems coming from areas outside them, such as philosophy and history. Biology, for instance, has to deal with philosophical problems about the concept of life and also with vast historical problems about evolution for which it uses historical methods, not those of physics. Moreover, the history of science itself is, as we shall see, extremely instructive, allowing us to understand crucial things about it that would otherwise be mysterious.

Physical science, then, is not a separate, supreme champion outclassing history or philosophy. It has no private line to reality. It is an immensely important range of studies with its own characteristic subject matter and it does not need to be flattered by being supposed to be universal. All sciences have their different kinds of work that must be done together. But, as just mentioned, this leads us to a still more interesting issue: why, then, is this particular study so exceptionally important? Why does it deserve cathedrals if other studies do not? In this world empty of conscious subjects, for whom does it have that value? Who, so to speak, wants and accepts and appreciates and consumes all this information? For whom does it matter? Whose life is it supposed to change?

The prophets of scientism do not tell us this. For them, the real world apparently consists only of objects; it contains no subjects. And the whole idea of an observer may be – as has been suggested in the case of quantum phenomena – simply a shorthand way of referring to the telescopes and the record. This, indeed, is the kind of thinking that leads to the wild conclusion that we ourselves are not there.

This situation is not easy to grasp because it really is new. Until quite lately, fresh claims about the priority of a particular study took place within a familiar context. They had to be related to similar claims about other human activities such as, for instance, love, religion, politics, sport, exploration and the arts. They had to be placed somewhere on a familiar map of social life. They might indeed be about to alter that familiar map by proposing a new balance, but they needed it for a start in order to explain their claims. Other possible claimants had to be noticed.

Today, however, Science tends to be exalted in isolation, as if any attempt to relate it to other valuable activities was anti-scientific. In this way the familiar imaginative map of values, along with the social feelings that generated it – the human fears and wishes that form our language about what is important – simply vanishes. Without this range of alternatives, praise and dispraise mean nothing and the whole idea of relative importance evaporates.

This myth is therefore not very helpful. In this book I shall discuss its history, the arguments that are used to support it and the range of real problems out of which it has grown. I shall, of course, look at some sensible arguments that have made people think in this sort of way. But I am anxious to point out here for a start that this idea of our own non-existence is a myth, not a solid scientific discovery. It is a recently proposed imaginative vision, one optional way among others of conceiving the world. And it really does not make sense.

This may be hard to grasp because (as we shall see) it is at present being propounded by actual scientists: people with the appropriate PhDs who work in labs, some of them indeed very distinguished. What this shows is that, unfortunately, scientific education has of late become very narrow. It doesn't direct people's attention half enough to understanding the meaning of what they are saying, in particular to the difference between our various ways of thinking. And what it hardly ever teaches them is to take notice of those deep assumptions that I just mentioned: the presuppositions that they are taking for granted.

This was not always so. Up to and including the generation of Niels Bohr and Albert Einstein, serious scientists always had a philosophical background and really studied the conceptual tangles that their theories involved. (T. H. Huxley was particularly keen on doing this, as was J. B. S. Haldane.) Bohr and Einstein themselves clearly knew about Kant's discussions of subjectivity and objectivity and used them in their own proposals. Soon after their time, however, both disciplines drew themselves in and narrowed their borders, learning to regard what was outside them as someone else's business.

Among other bad consequences, this has also led some philosophers such as Daniel Dennett to take seriously the anti-self doctrines that we shall discuss in this book, assuming them to be scientific. I have not followed their discussions here because, although they add plenty of subtlety, they don't in my view alter the central issue, which concerns the basic presuppositions that we live by. The plain wording of the scientists sticks closer to these presuppositions, so I have usually concentrated on it.

The book is circular rather than linear. It goes all round its subject. Because the strange phenomenon of selficide or the destruction of the soul poses so many different kinds of problems, I have tried to explore it from a number of different angles.

Thus, besides investigating our current attitudes to individuals, including ourselves, and especially to the ways in which those individuals seem to be divided, I have paid a lot of attention to the sources of these attitudes: to the deep and lasting traditions from which they stem. In doing this I have had to leap frequently between past and present, and I can only hope that I have not made that process too confusing,

Readers who can't stand history are welcome to skip Chapters 3 and 12. Doing this will, however, probably deprive them of a lot of fun, and of some insights that are really relevant to the present day.

1

CHANGING RELATIONS TO THE COSMOS

MIND AND BODY?

We have noticed that these deep presuppositions of our thought are subject to constant stirs and struggles, causing serious alterations in what we now count as science. These shifts sometimes pass unnoticed because they are gradual, but sometimes they break out into catastrophic earthquakes. Thus science is not immutable. If you haven't lived through one of these earthquakes it can be quite hard to believe in them – hard, in particular, to believe that people can have been so stupid as to accept what they seem to have accepted before the most recent change. But that is how things go. We need to be alive to the possibility that some current assumptions will simply turn out wrong.

One of these earthquakes notoriously took place in the seventeenth century with Isaac Newton and the dawn of modern

DOI: 10.4324/9781003411710-2

science. Another followed it a couple of centuries ago, early in the nineteenth century, when that Newtonian orthodoxy was finally forced to admit temporal change – evolution – into a world that had been thought of as fixed and eternal. This advance into the realm of time and change was disturbing enough, but it was only part of a larger shift that was arising in the orthodox worldview. Modern science, which had been so triumphantly founded on that worldview in the seventeenth century -

> Nature and Nature's laws lay hid in night.
> God said, *Let Newton be!* and all was light.

as Alexander Pope put it – found that its assumptions no longer seemed to fit the world quite as well as they had. Apparently it needed to think again. It still does.

Besides the incursion of time, trouble was beginning to arise about the relation between mind and body. Here the orthodox view required dualism: the belief in a world made up ultimately of spirit and matter. Spirit was the primary force, providing both a central organizer – God, who generated the eternal order – and a mental space in which the inner life of humans could go on. Matter, by contrast, was a minor partner. It was taken to be a set of inert, neutral particles without qualities: mere raw material for active spirit to work on.

And for some time this picture remained usable. But the idea of spirit, which did so much work in it, was unfortunately linked to the churches, which became politically unpopular because they were involved in religious wars. Literal interpretation of the Bible was being undermined by historical evidence. Great efforts were therefore made to analyse the world in a safer, less subjective way – to provide a new conceptual drama and a fresh cast of ideas. Even people who still accepted the religious message of the Bible saw that some such new background story was needed.

Disputes centred at first chiefly on finding a new organizing force to replace God. And that creative role was conferred on natural selection, which, despite increasing difficulties about matters like the origin of life (which we shall need to discuss later) is still held to occupy it today.

By contrast, questions about subjectivity – about the soul or spirit – did not seriously arise until the start of the twentieth century. At that time behaviourist psychologists suddenly ruled that consciousness must be banished from academic consideration altogether because it was unscientific. A scientific psychology must deal only with movements of physical matter: that is, behaviour. They thus launched their own mini-earthquake, which has turned out remarkably influential. They campaigned vigorously to solve the mind–body problem by removing the mind. That campaign is still rampant today and will occupy much of this book.

WHO IS PRESENT?

Are souls – spirits, subjects, selves, minds – actually just an optional extra that can be dropped without inconvenience, or do they do vital work? Are they perhaps indeed a vital axis in our lives?

This is not an isolated issue. It carries with it still wider questions – questions about how we should conceive the whole universe that contains us and the sciences that study it. As Thomas Nagel puts it:

> it is important both for science itself and for philosophy to ask *how much of what there is the physical sciences can render intelligible* – how much of the world's intelligibility consists in its subsumability under universal, mathematically formulable

laws governing the spatiotemporal order. If there are limits to the reach of science in this form, are there other forms of understanding that can render intelligible what physical science does not explain?...

My guiding conviction is that *mind is not just an afterthought or an accident or an add-on, but a basic aspect of nature....*

The intelligibility of the world is no accident.

(2012: 18, 16, 17, emphasis added)

In short, our notion of what we ourselves are is not a marginal item that we can alter to suit a fashion. It forms part of our idea of what the universe itself is and the two must fit together. Nagel's proposal calls in question some ideas that have long formed an unstated dominant credo among academics, ideas that display physical science as a kind of sun at the centre of the intellectual cosmos and mind as just an inconvenient peripheral planet that may, with luck, finally be excluded from that system altogether.

Nagel deliberately affronted that credo by calling his book *Mind and Cosmos: Why the Materialist Neo-Darwinian Conception of Nature is Almost Certainly False.* So the book caused some little alarm. Even though the credo itself is already beginning to fray around the edges, people who think of themselves as scientifically oriented still often revere materialism in much the same way that their predecessors in Darwin's day revered Christianity. That is, they don't ask questions about it but view it as the general background against which all decent disputes must take place. They often assume that the only reasons for questioning it would be religious ones, probably flowing from creationism.

But in truth the main difficulties here have nothing to do with religion. They arise because, since the elements of this concept were formed three centuries ago, many things have changed so drastically that the whole idea of materialism has become deeply obscure. As we shall see, the central trouble is that the conception of *matter* has remained essentially unchanged since the seventeenth century, while the load of work that it is expected to do has increased dramatically and the concepts that used to share the burden have gone.

In particular, our current belief in our evolutionary origin calls for matter to take over the burden of creation. For this to work, matter must always, from the start, have had in it the potentiality for life – and indeed for mind – along with tendencies to implement that potentiality. If, indeed, the Lord did not interfere, how, without that potentiality, could this vast show ever have got on the road?

Even the physical difficulties facing this enterprise seem bad enough. As the cosmologist Paul Davies puts it: "For life to emerge, and then to evolve into conscious beings like ourselves":

> certain stringent conditions must be satisfied in the underlying laws of physics that regulate the universe, so stringent in fact that a bio-friendly universe looks like a fix — or "a put-up job"... On the face of it, the universe *does* look as if it has been designed by an intelligent creator expressly for the purpose of spawning sentient beings. Like the porridge in the tale of Goldilocks and the three bears, the universe seems to be "just right" for life, in many intriguing ways.
>
> *(2006: 2–3)*

But, once this habitable world is there, how come there is somebody present to take advantage of it? Simon Conway Morris comments:

> At the heart of the study of evolution are two things. One... is the uncanny ability of evolution to navigate to the appropriate

> solution though immense "hyperspaces" of biological possi-
> bility. The other, equally germane and even more mysterious,
> is the attempt to explain the origins of sentience, such that the
> product of ultimately inanimate processes can come to under-
> stand... itself, its world and... its (and thus our) strange sense
> of purpose.
>
> *(2003: 327)*

To show how species "navigate to the appropriate solution" Conway Morris points to the remarkable prevalence of evolutionary convergence: cases where unrelated organisms have quite separately come up with the same sophisticated device. Eight distinct kinds of creature, for instance, have separately developed eyes, and the very complex kind of camera-eye that we use is also used by those very distant relatives the squids and octopuses. Similar striking convergences are found in the other sense-organs and also in those that preserve balance. If evolution really proceeded by random leaps this sort of thing could never happen. What emerges appears to be a bias in evolution towards finding solutions that make directed, intelligent life more possible and easier.

These convergences have usually been treated as mere coincidences but they are really too frequent for that. What is happening seems to be some kind of self-organization. And this, of course, could not happen if evolution were simply a machine run by the genes. However, it was already becoming clear that it is *not* such a machine; that the genes are not always (as people say) in the driving seat. Recent work on epigenetics – the effect of life experience on the way in which genes are expressed – has shown that considerable changes are possible, and some biologists are now exploring the possibility that creatures' individual choices of lifestyle may really promote these changes towards better perception. This is not, of course, Jean-Baptiste

Lamarck's suggestion that behaviour directly changes body form; it proceeds through shifts in gene-expression (Holmes 2013a: 33).

About all these things physics can tell us nothing. The idea of natural selection, which, as we shall see, is usually called in to account for this vast creative surge, is already looking increasingly inadequate to explain evolution. The main trouble with it is, I think, best explained in the analogy of coffee. Natural selection is only a filter, and filters do not provide the taste of the coffee that pours through them. Similarly, the range of evolutionary alternatives between which selection takes place has to be there already in matter. How it comes to be present there is the real mystery about creation.

Meanwhile the notion of spirit – which used to be credited with the rest of this creative work – has been dismissed altogether from science. This dismissal is part of a wider process in which all intellectual disciplines have been gradually splitting up and becoming more specialized, so that they often cannot accommodate these big topics and drop the concepts that would be appropriate for them.

Yet the big topics still need to be discussed; indeed, if anything, they get more urgent and more difficult from being neglected. Philosophy, which used to take responsibility for these interdisciplinary matters, has unfortunately chosen to regard itself as just one more limited discipline and has largely followed the academic fashion of becoming increasingly technical and preferring smaller questions. But Nagel – who, incidentally, does not himself carry any religious message – has always insisted on discussing big, difficult issues and his proposals about them here are surely helpful.

Nagel's main message in *Mind and Cosmos* is that a cosmos that contains conscious, thinking beings like ourselves must be different from one that does not contain them – so different that it cannot be described in the same terms. Physics and chemistry are abstract systems admirably devised for describing unconscious substances, and they do this very well. It is surely unwise to use them on subject matter like this, which does not suit them.

THE TABOO ON CONSCIOUNESS

That unwise policy, however, is prevalent today because it was the gospel preached with great effect, about a century ago, by those influential prophets, the behaviourists, who may indeed have been the first people to use the word *scientific* with the strong campaigning force that it still bears today – to imply that whatever does not follow the supposed methods of physical science cannot be a proper part of reasoning at all.

These behaviourists were American psychologists who, in response to some unsatisfactory attempts by other theorists to examine the mind through introspection, declared that psychology must abandon all talk of inner mental experience altogether. This study, they said, should only be a straightforward examination of outward behaviour, which could, they hoped, eventually be viewed as a satisfactory extension of physical science. They did not actually deny that consciousness occurs. They just said it was a meaningless by-product of behaviour, something that had no effect on subsequent actions. (This idea that something could have physical causes but no physical effects is rather a strange one, as we shall see when we discuss it later, in Chapter 9.) Psychologists, they said, should therefore ignore it. And people who talked about unconscious motivation, as Sigmund Freud and William James did, were merely wasting their time. Motivation, in fact, became altogether a non-subject.

This should, of course, have meant that all the rest of the syllabus outside science – history, linguistics, philosophy, poetry, logic, geography, law, mathematics and indeed most of the social sciences – should be banished entirely from academe. The behaviourists liked this idea, but their main aim was to shoot down more limited targets: their own rivals in the social sciences, especially other psychologists who drew attention to the inner life. And within that circle they were, for a time, extraordinarily successful, successful in a way that shows how strong and irrational the special prestige attached to the name of science had already become.

The very word "science", which had originally meant knowledge or understanding in general, gradually became narrowed during the nineteenth century to mean only physical science. This made it possible for the behaviourists to persuade social scientists generally that they should ignore the non-physical aspects of human life. In particular, if possible they should not even think about such disreputable matters as consciousness and emotion, and, if they did, they should keep silent for the sake of their careers.

Behaviourist investigations themselves escaped this ban because the "behaviour patterns" they dealt in were supposed to be seen as simply objective physical phenomena. And, although much of this research turned out not to be very useful, the horror of subjectivity that had been drilled into the social sciences has proved lasting. The idea has spread that talking about subjectivity is itself subjective: that, if you want to be *objective* (that is, fair), you must talk only about *objects*, never about subjects.

This is clearly a wild principle. It seems to be the same maxim that Dr Johnson caricatured when he suggested that "who drives fat oxen should himself be fat". That, however, has not made it any less persuasive. It has even spread to many parts of the humanities, where historians and philosophers struggle sternly to conceal their own interests and personalities behind a screen of graphs and statistics, vainly hoping that this will make them look as impersonal as physicists.

Since many people who choose to study the social sciences do so just because they are deeply interested in the human heart, this convention of pretending to ignore hearts has led to a great deal of anxiety and bad faith. It generates pseudo-scientific superstitions, doctrines professed for the sake of appearances but not seriously believable. Prominent among these is the story that is the central theme of this book: that Science has shown our inner selves to be illusory.

Unkind observers sometimes enquire who, in that case, actually writes the books that expound this doctrine? Do the brain cells really do this work on their own? But, as we shall see, these ideas are not just accidental froth; they arise from serious trends in our culture's history. The current stream of our thought is like a river that has been gradually shifted from its former course by accumulations of silt and is now flowing in very odd directions. We need to attend to them. What do they mean?

These recent shifts have left many of us convinced that our mental life should somehow be studied by the physical sciences, but with no usable methods by which those sciences can handle it. (This, of course, is one reason why people are proposing to get rid of mental life altogether.) Besides this, however, these shifts have also left us in a very bizarre and paradoxical relation to the material world that those sciences do handle.

The reasons that used to be given why the material world should concern us no longer seem to apply. We do not now see that world, as our seventeenth-century forebears did, as God's creation, an expression of his glorious vision, a book to be eagerly studied (as Newton said) in order to understand the depths of God's thought. Without that background and without the older, spontaneous reverence for the earth as our nourishing mother – without anything like the Homeric Hymn to Gaia – this physical world is surely just a mass of stuff. Of course, we need to control it for reasons of convenience, and we may choose to investigate it as an exercise to stop our mental faculties from getting rusty. But in itself, from the materialist point of view that we are considering, it surely has no value. Why, then, bother with examining it at all?

This notion is so far from the attitude of most great scientists, both past and present – so hostile to the kind of sensibility that commonly leads people to study science – that its being plausible today surely shows us that something is wrong. What, then, has been happening to the idea of science?

2

SCIENCEPHOBIA AND ITS SOURCES

ARE YOU NOTHING?

Let us start this enquiry by asking: what is it that frightens people today so much about Science? How can such a useful study – one that gives us many of the facts on which we build our lives – sometimes strike ordinary people as an alien and destructive force?

This is not just due to traditional clashes between science and religion. Those clashes have often yielded to further thought, and anyway religion itself – at least in the United Kingdom – is less central to our lives than it once was. What remains now, and is far more disturbing, is a certain anti-human attitude that seems to be associated with Science: a claim that Science has disproved beliefs that we need for ordinary life; that it shows up our ordinary attitudes as worthless because they are unscientific.

DOI: 10.4324/9781003411710-3

A striking part of that claim is this doctrine that our inner selves, as we experience them, don't really exist at all. The question is now not just "Do you believe in God?", but – what is surely more alarming – "Do you believe in yourself?" This idea has been floating around for some time and has had some very distinguished supporters. Besides some philosophers, whose views don't often reach the general public, Francis Crick (Mr DNA himself) told us sternly twenty years ago in his book *The Astonishing Hypothesis* that: "'You,' your joys and your sorrows, your memories and your ambitions, your sense of personal identity and free will, are in fact no more than the behaviour of a vast assembly of nerve cells and their attendant molecules" (1994: 3, emphasis added).

What does this mean? An unsophisticated reader might naturally hear it as a straightforward insult. And in fact the cyber-bullies who currently torment children apparently like to say exactly this: "You are nothing". Another possibility, which we will have to consider later, is that it really means "Don't let talk about these personal matters interfere with your work; they are irrelevant to your professional business". The suggestion here is that the truth at which science aims is an isolated one, separated from all the affairs of everyday life: an abstract Truth, unpolluted by vulgar details. We shall ask what this means in Chapters 3 and 12. What Crick and his followers actually mean by it is not at once clear but officially it seems to be something quite close to this second possibility, namely, that our consciousness is not real because the only real things in the world are those revealed by the physical sciences. He does not discuss evidence for this and it certainly looks like a wild philosophical speculation, but he assures us that it has somehow been scientifically established:

> The *scientific belief* is that our minds – the behavior of our brains – can be *explained* by the interaction of nerve cells

(and other cells) and the molecules associated with them. This is to most people a really surprising concept. It does not come easily to believe *that I am the detailed behaviour of a set of nerve cells.*

(Ibid.: 7, emphasis added)

Similarly, the neuroscientist Susan Greenfield, looking at an exposed brain in an operating theatre, reflected that, "This was all there was to Sarah, or indeed to any of us... We are but sludgy brains" (2000: 12) and the eminent neurophysiologist Colin Blakemore writes:

The human brain is a machine which *alone accounts for all our actions*, our most private thoughts, our beliefs... *All our actions are products of the activity of our brains*. It makes no sense (in scientific terms) to distinguish sharply between acts that result from conscious attention and those that result from our reflexes or damage to the brain.

(1999: 270, emphases added)

Thus, if we want to understand why (for instance) Napoleon decided to invade Egypt or Russia, what we need is not – as we might think – some knowledge of the political background and of Napoleon's state of mind, but simply facts about the state of his brain, which alone can account for his action. Nor can any question even be raised about how far he was responsible for these invasions.

ON BEING A NECESSARY ILLUSION

This is not a very intelligible story. It has, however, become amazingly widely accepted today among respectable scientists, as can be seen from a special issue of the prestigious magazine

New Scientist on 23 February 2013. Here, half a dozen authors who clearly feel no need to justify their strange positions assure us that, although the "intuitive sense of self is an effortless and fundamental human experience", it is still "nothing more than an *elaborate illusion*... Some thinkers even go so far as claiming that there is *no such thing as the self*" (*New Scientist* 2013: 33, emphases added). "You are being *tricked* into thinking that you live in the present" (Westerhoff 2013b: 37) "your self can even be *tricked* into hovering in mid-air outside the body" (Ananthaswamy & Lawton 2013: 40). (So apparently it is real enough to be tricked; is that not odd?) And again – "Much of what we take for granted about our inner lives, from visual perception to memories, is little more than an elaborate *construct of the mind* [sic]. The self is just another part of this illusion" (Fisher 2013: 43, emphasis added). (Here, remarkably, the mind makes things still harder by appearing as both deceiver and deceived.)

If we are to understand this surprising piece of news we surely need to know what it means. It should be made clear right away that this is *not* the Buddhist doctrine of no-self. That doctrine starts with the same destructive step of rejecting the substantial, immortal self of tradition, but it does so in order to deploy a quite different, richer and more subtle worldview: one that calls for a distinctive life, dedicated to consideration for others and understanding of the ultimate mysteries; one in which we would identify primarily with a much larger whole. The kind of exclusive materialism that we are now considering makes absolutely no such constructive suggestion. It does not even explain whether accepting our non-existence is supposed to make us change our lives at all. At first it seems that it may well do so:

> Many of our core beliefs about ourselves do not withstand scru-
> tiny. This presents a tremendous challenge for our everyday

view of ourselves, as it suggests that in a very fundamental way
we are not real. Instead, our self is comparable to an illusion –
but without anybody there that experiences the illusion.

(Westerhoff 2013a: 37)

But later all this turns out not to matter in the least. The same
writer goes on to say "Yet we may have no choice but to en-
dorse these mistaken beliefs... *The self is not only a useful illusion, it
may also be a necessary one*" (ibid., emphasis added). So apparently
things should go on just as they are.

SOME QUERIES

These are surely very odd claims. In the first place, we naturally
ask just who it is that is being thus deluded? Illusions don't
float about in mid-air; somebody has to entertain them. This
was one thing that Descartes got right. As he pointed out, you
can't be mistaken if you aren't there in the first place. "Deceive
me who may," cried Descartes in his *Second Meditation*, "he cannot
bring it about that I who am deceived do not exist". And that
still seems to hold.

Then again, scientists are not supposed to tell lies, so what is
meant by saying that we must accept a falsehood here because
it is useful and necessary? Normally, talk of "useful illusions"
refers to false beliefs that we want *other people* to hold, beliefs
such as the public's conviction that its rulers are acting respon-
sibly. But here we are being asked to accept lies ourselves while
still knowing them to be lies. How would that work?

That question has a wider application because this way of
saving oneself the trouble of answering unwelcome opinions
by claiming that they are just tricks played on us by evolution
is at present increasingly widespread. As we shall see, it is now
standardly used about free will and very often too about religion. We shall have to come back to it later.

It is puzzling, too, that this illusory self has now acquired an author – an active deceiver – as is clearly implied by words like "tricked" and "elaborate". Wasn't the whole point of this move to get rid of active agents?

And again, what does Greenfield mean by saying, "this was all there was to Sarah"? If we ask "who is this Sarah?", will the answer be "well of course, like everybody else, she is just a standard mass of brain cells and molecules – although I believe her hippocampus does have an interesting twist round towards the right"? Or might our informant add "Oh yes, and I believe her surname was Palin or something like that"? Or perhaps not? And then again, how is this selficide supposed to relate to the current emphasis among biologists on selfishness as an evolutionary force, or indeed to the general individualistic flavour that pervades today's political thinking?

It also seems remarkable that Crick and his followers are quite satisfied with the reality of brain cells. Why do they not pursue their reductive course right down to quarks or electrons, or whatever may be today's currently favoured physical terminus? In view of this hesitation, we can reasonably ask, what is the actual aim of this reductive journey? As we shall see in Chapter 12, the belief that lies behind this way of thinking is that only physics itself, not just physical science generally, can put us in touch with reality. And, although the roots of this idea are ancient and profoundly religious, they seem to be the only ones that could get us to this kind of position.

There is, too, the rather obstinate issue of pain. Certainly Christian Scientists and some other sages have told us that pain too is an illusion, and by doing this they have sometimes actually managed to mitigate people's suffering. They have shown that attention really is important here, which is a valuable and helpful insight. But the effects of shifting one's attention are limited and it is hard to see what on earth it could mean to suggest that, after that shifting, the remaining suffering is unreal. The old limerick probably puts this point best:

> There was a faith-healer of Deal
> Who said, "Although pain isn't real,
> If I sit on a pin
> And it punctures my skin
> I dislike what I fancy I feel".

In fact, the whole idea of illusion seems to make sense only if we accept the reality of the illusory experience as an experience and question only what it seems to be telling us about the outside world. Optical illusions do really happen. What they can't do is provide accurate measurements of the outside world. The idea of having, so to speak, two successive layers of illusion here is unworkable.

REDUCTION AND TECHNICAL LANGUAGE

We shall look into these various oddities later. But this last point about the meaning of reduction surely brings us to the nub of the difficulty: the strange notion of illusion and reality that is involved here.

Accounts such as Crick's tell us that the language used in the physical sciences trumps the language of everyday life in a crucial way. This technical language is (they say) not just more suited to certain detailed enquiries than ordinary speech but it is ontologically superior – closer to reality. It alone can tell the truth. Other languages deal only in illusion.

Now this is a big change from the earlier stages of scientific development. When the questions being asked were about such things as the flatness of the earth it was clear that the clash was not between different languages but between different views of the facts. Both views could (if necessary) be expressed in either language. And for quite a large part of that development such translation was still possible because the technical language had not moved too far away from the ordinary point of view.

After a time, however, as particular technical languages became more arcane and dealt in increasingly specialized topics – as has now happened with neurology – this direct translation stopped being possible. The relation between the two subject matters needs then to be explicitly stated and thought about. But there is still no reason to expect that one of their messages will turn out to be real and the other illusory. These two languages are not rivals, competitors for a prize marked "reality". They merely do different work. Their differences simply show that when we talk about the same topic, we are considering it from different angles and asking different questions. There need be no suspicion that either account is illusory unless we see something that really indicates fishiness.

If, for instance, I am looking down over the parapet of Westminster Bridge and I say "Well, so that is the Thames", it is not appropriate for you to reply "No, actually you're wrong, that's a mistake people often make. These names that are given to rivers are a mere superstition, you know. That is really just H_2O with certain well-recognized impurities."

Of course there are situations in which this sort of comment would be quite appropriate: for instance if somebody wants to walk on the Thames or to take their drinking water from it. But these are familiar, well-signed turning points in conversation: times when we already know that we have to shift to a different kind of language. That shift may be needed to correct ordinary factual mistakes or merely to make things clearer, but it can never stigmatize a whole point of view – which is otherwise being successfully used – as being illusory.

ATOMS AND WHOLES

Why, then, have these drastic reductive stories developed and why do people find them so convincing? The trouble seems again to have been excessive enthusiasm, making it hard to know when to stop using something that has worked well so far. As we saw, Science has acquired great authority because people repeatedly found that it had indeed increased their knowledge. It was natural to expect that this good work would continue indefinitely.

What blocked this hopeful process, however, was increasing specialization. As scientific studies became more detailed, it grew harder and harder to connect their findings intelligibly with everyday life. People's loyalty therefore shifted to the more general presuppositions that lay behind these details: the deeper assumptions that, as we saw earlier, commonly determine which questions we ask, and assumptions which can influence general thought far beyond the technical points that first gave rise to them. These assumptions are, of course, often counted as part of science. But, as we have seen, they often need to be changed.

A particularly strong assumption here has been scientists' deep reliance on atomization: on finding the meaning of things by breaking them down into their smallest components. Atomization illustrates the simplest, most literal meaning of the word "reduction"; it works by making things smaller. The illumination that follows does not, of course, flow simply from their being smaller but from the wider scientific picture into which they have now been fitted. That picture gives them a new kind of context, a wider whole within which they can be differently understood. And finding that kind of context is an essential part of what "understanding" means.

Each method can, however, throw that light only on problems of the kind that picture is fitted to deal with. And there is certainly no reason why these units should be considered any more real than the things they compose. A microscope is a wonderful machine, but that does not make what is seen through it any more real than the things outside.

The atomizing method has, of course, been hugely useful in discovering the structure of physical matter and in such well-fitting contexts it is an unparalleled intellectual tool. But all such tools work only in their proper place. It is no use refusing to use anything but a chisel. When nineteenth-century psychologists tried to follow this method by looking for the ultimate units of thought they got nowhere. Thought doesn't come in units: it's continuous. My example of the Thames is meant to show in simple form how things go wrong when people concentrate on atomic units without considering the wholes they belong to. The mistake that typically grows from the atomistic assumption is neglecting these wholes, supposing that they are somehow unreal or secondary to their parts. This mistake is much encouraged by the metaphor of bricks or "building-blocks", which strongly suggests a pile of these simple items present at the start, only needing to be put together.

But, as we know, the world has never been like that. As soon as anything solid appeared at all it took the form of complex, mixed-up entities that grew into more of the same. And, as Nagel pointed out long ago (Nagel 1979) these entities must already have had in them the potentiality of forming into the living and conscious beings that developed later. Since no bricklayer was present to build them into organisms they must have done it themselves. It was self-organization. But that is a story of which physics says nothing.

Among the entities that resulted are rivers, which it is entirely rational to consider as wholes: solid, structured facts in the world, involving geographical and historical details of their own that are as objective as anything in physics. The point of naming them is to place them within yet wider wholes such as nations and continents so as to record their role in history and to gain understanding of larger geographical facts. This preliminary outward movement of thought – holism – is every bit as necessary as the inward, atomizing one and in any investigation it usually needs to come first.

In this way the case of rivers seems to me quite like that of individual human beings. Like rivers, human beings too are given names to make clear their relations to the various systems round them in the world. As they act in these systems, the details of their thoughts and feelings are no less real and effective than the details about their brain cells (or indeed about their genes). The chief difference between humans and rivers is that humans are an immeasurably more complex kind of entity, so that in their case it is even less useful to suppose that they can be fully explained reductively in terms of particular physical parts or of a single physical science.

The chief source of such mistakes is, I think, a general overconfidence in the reductive method, but the trouble has been much increased by a parallel change in the concept of science itself. That word used to have quite a wide meaning covering *understanding* or *knowledge* generally, and it still often does so. For instance until lately the University of Cambridge had a course called "moral sciences", which meant social sciences and philosophy. For quite a long time now, however, the word *science* has been narrowing its sense so as to mean primarily physical science, and at present a further narrowing is in progress to treat it as meaning simply physics (with chemistry as a minor adjunct). That is because physics is seen as dealing with the most fundamental objects: the "ultimate building-blocks of reality".

This has quite a large effect on the notion of materialism we are now considering. That word (when it isn't just being used to stand for an obsession with profit) is usually taken to mean something like "nothing is real except the physical objects that are described by the natural sciences". Its central emphasis is negative; the point is that there is no such thing as what used to be called spirit.

Many people who think they are materialists may therefore well suppose that "materialism" adequately describes the world they live in. That world consists (they think) of everyday objects such as houses and apples, air and water: items that are, after all, fit topics for natural science in its old sense. But if we take *science* to mean simply physics, as some people now suggest, all this must change. We are then in an arctic world of abstractions, a world of particles, forces and fields, where no concrete things like apples and houses are ever conceived of – a world in which, although air may be present, it will certainly not be breathed, since breathing is a strictly biological activity. There is certainly no place for life. It is not clear, therefore, how – on this view – Crick and his colleagues could find room there for their brain cells, or even their biologically conditioned molecules.

This question about the central role of physics is increasingly important today because theorists are insisting that *materialism* is equivalent to *physicalism*. It is not always clear that they have noticed how much this formula might change the world they inhabit. The main trouble is that the word *physical* has shifted its meaning. It used to be seen chiefly as the opposite of *supernatural*, so that theorists classed themselves as physicalists primarily to show that they did not consider God as a cause of earthly events, a point they could also make by claiming to be *naturalists*.

In recent times, however, since these metaphysical debates had become less widespread, *physical* came to be used much more often as the opposite of *mental*, as it is when we talk of "mental and physical symptoms". This change made it natural for people who wanted to get rid of the mind to call themselves physicalists in a quite different sense, meaning simply that they don't believe there is anything mental.

Galen Strawson, who has long been an ardent naturalist and physicalist in the old sense, has written a furious article in the *London Review of Books* denouncing this shift as wild and meaningless. He points out (rightly) that earlier philosophers who called themselves naturalists and physicalists never drew such conclusions. The trouble has arisen, he says, because the behaviourists' perfectly proper emphasis on the role of outside behaviour:

> turned into a mad metaphysical thesis in philosophy according to which there is nothing more to experience than behaviour and dispositions to behaviour; i.e., bluntly put, experience doesn't really exist. Things got worse... The denial of the existence of experience came to be thought of as naturalistic independently of any behaviourist (or "functionalist") assumptions. The dubious existence or non-existence of experience was thought to follow simply from the fact – the view – that everything is wholly physical.
>
> *(Strawson 2013: 28; see also Strawson 2008)*

What can be done about all this? The unlucky word *physical* is, of course, only the Greek form of the word *natural* and it gets different meanings according to the various ways in which people conceive nature – in particular, according to what they want to contrast nature with at the time. But today the public glorification of physics is likely to encourage the simple idea people like Wolpert have expressed (see pp. 148–9): that this hugely abstract set of methods is indeed our supreme study, our only window on reality. As Wolpert puts it, "all science aspires to be like physics" (1992: 121).

This really is an empty suggestion. It is relevant to ask, as Nagel does in the passage already quoted, "how much of the world's intelligibility consists in its subsumability under universal, mathematically formulable laws governing the spatiotemporal order" (2012: 18): "If life is not just a physical phenomenon, the origin and evolution of life and mind will not be explainable by physics and chemistry alone" (ibid.: 33).

Well, plainly, some tools for new forms of understanding already exist, many of them now classed as parts of the humanities, where they range from law through philosophy to poetry. Obvious candidates among these sets of tools are the methods of philosophy and history, about which Nagel comments:

> We stand in need of both a constitutive explanation of what rationality might consist in and a historical explanation of how it arose; and both explanations must be consistent with our being, among other things, physical organisms. The understanding of biological organisms and their evolutionary history would have to expand to accommodate this additional explanatory burden, as I have argued it must expand beyond materialism to accommodate the explanation of consciousness.
>
> *(Ibid.: 86)*

In short, in an age when all intellectual disciplines are shrinking their scope to become increasingly specialized it is not possible for any single department of thought to expect to handle large questions on its own. If we are to deal with large questions at all we shall have to do it by combining several kinds of tool: several different methods belonging to different disciplines.

MULTITUDES WITHIN

Doing this need not involve a hopeless clash. The difficulty is sometimes no greater than it would be if we found that we have to use several languages, something that can, of course, at times be troublesome enough but which usually yields to practice. At other times, however, there really are great mental distances to be covered and serious work is needed to bring the various elements together.

Sometimes the two modes of thinking are distant because they belong to different thought-worlds: two distinct cultures, distinct ways of envisaging life. This, indeed, constantly happens today when a worldview accepted in the West has to be brought together with one from a different tradition. But what is still more surprising is that at other times the difference is not due to their having separate origins at all. Sometimes the two incompatible approaches are combined within a single life, and they may have lived there together in some kind of harmony ever since that life began. In fact, perfectly normal citizens can live by two or more distinct strategies that disagree so drastically that anyone could see the clash if they were explicitly spelt out, but, with remarkable skill, this exposure is usually avoided.

This kind of divided worldview is, of course, most conspicuous in extreme cases such as the concentration-camp guards who apparently were humane and sympathetic fathers of families at home without being disturbed by this in their inhumane behaviour at work. In ordinary social life the division usually takes milder forms, but still a clash is often visible and to some extent admitted. It can start early in life. A child who starts to go to school often responds to the school's customs by developing a distinct school personality and using a slightly different language. Where the difference is not too great the school personality can be satisfactorily merged with the out-of-school personality, but when seriously distinct worlds are clashing the split is liable to become chronic, although it may still not be explicitly recognized.

On top of this there are, of course, differences between the attitudes of the parents and the other people around, as well as conflicts within the personalities of each of them. All this is before the family runs into any serious change, such as breaking up or moving to somewhere socially different, and before we start to think about gaps in later life between attitudes at home and at work. Altogether, it is not surprising if inner conflict is a fairly normal human condition.

And so it comes about that, as we all know, grown-up citizens – often highly educated – can profess and apparently believe two or more sets of doctrines that flatly contradict each other. Marxism, when it was fashionable, used to provide a particularly fertile field for such arrangements because its dialectic supplied reputable ways of combining opposites. But the current unfashionableness of Marxism has certainly not made these inner divisions less common; it just means that people take less trouble now to understand them. Perhaps most of us carry elements of such problems about with us. For instance, most of us non-vegan animal-lovers have a divided attitude to our fellow creatures.

This conflictedness is not a disaster provided we know that it is on its way to being cured. At some level, we need to see these clashes as part of a process: a developing dialectic in which various useful aspects of life are growing up in parallel, so that the best elements in them can finally join to form something more harmonious. Hegel's idea of thesis and antithesis growing to form a synthesis is often really useful here; we are always working towards a reconciliation.

If, however, this dynamic dies – if the conflict stops being seen as temporary – if the embattled person canonizes one of the contenders in a way that makes all change unthinkable – then the real trouble begins. Then we are drifting towards disaster and a disaster of a very destructive kind. The trouble is not just the inconvenience of trying to follow two policies that continually frustrate each other. It is the deeper misfortune of lacking a guiding centre to one's life: of never really knowing what matters most.

This is the danger that I suggest threatens the kind of exclusive materialism we have been discussing. Something that is believed to be science is clashing here with the irremovable practical principles by which we live our lives. And its case is particularly awkward because of the special sort of priority that is felt to attach to science.

We are quite used to seeing people (other people, of course) accept and live with inner conflict about political or religious doctrines that we ourselves don't accept because we know that it is possible to hold contradictory beliefs on these matters. In science, however, we don't expect this to happen. Science is believed to deal only in proven facts, so its verdicts are taken to be final. In short, many of us "believe in" science in rather the way that people used to believe – and of course many, including some scientists, still do believe – in God. This kind of faith is not at all disturbed by the endless disputes that actually fragment the sciences.

We have seen that, behind these proven scientific facts, there are always hidden assumptions that from time to time need to be challenged. They can't remain immutable because they are a part of human culture. And in our history the assumptions that lie behind science have indeed often changed. We shall need to trace some of these shifts later. But it is probably worthwhile to glance briefly here at one of the most dramatic of them: the changing status of Almighty God himself.

Newton, Galileo, Boyle, Bacon and the other pioneers of modern science regarded God's reality not just as a given but as the central axis of their world system. As we shall see, they were particularly concerned to emphasize his total sovereignty so as to eliminate more pagan-seeming and possibly competing powers such as Mother Nature. The physics that they envisaged was conceived as essentially an expression of God's plan and they worked out its details in ways designed to give him due credit and honour. Today, by contrast, there are many people, both inside and outside science, who see belief in God not as part of science, but as flatly contrary to it: people who view Science and Religion as irreconcilable opposites. That is the scale on which change goes on. And that is why it is so important for us to understand it.

This apparent successful campaign of deicide is surely what has inspired the similar campaign that we are now discussing: the attempt to eliminate the human soul. This enterprise, which has developed during the past half century, is evidently intended to continue the same work of intellectual spring-cleaning. It is meant as one more hygienic use of Occam's razor, one more battle against the political power of the churches. And since souls are indeed a central topic of Christian teaching, that thought is entirely understandable. However, this move runs into difficulties that did not affect its predecessor, difficulties that, as we have seen, centre on the awkwardness of self-elimination. It is known to be possible to live without believing in God, but what would it mean to live without believing in oneself – indeed, to become absent?

Since actual suicide is apparently not being suggested, the idea must be that we should still survive but should think of ourselves differently, should penetrate behind appearances to realities that we now ignore. At first this sounds like the familiar change that we have to make when we find that we have been deceiving ourselves. For instance, if we have been thinking complacently about our past acts and then realize that we have actually been in the wrong, we can change our ideas and thereby our future behaviour. But if, instead of detecting past mistakes, we simply start contemplating the movements of our neurones, we shall clearly not have improved the situation. We shall not in any way have a better grasp of reality. We shall simply have shifted to thinking about something quite different.

What, then, is the supposed illusion? It cannot just be the experience of thinking; that experience is not an illusion, it is a fact. What is supposed to be illusory here is not the thinking itself but our impression that this thinking can affect the world. In short, as Crick mentions, the trouble is about free will: free will considered not as a general licence to escape causality but, as we normally understand the word, as a sense that our efforts can be genuinely effective.

The materialist credo rules that thoughts, not being physical, cannot cause physical events. And as we know from every activity of our lives that thoughts actually can and do affect those events – that they are often all too effective, producing practical results in the world even when we wish they wouldn't – this doctrine puts materialism into a radical conflict with reality. It operates as a kind of myth, enabling us to detach our scientific beliefs safely from our practical lives and to railroad psychological problems away from our thoughts by turning them over to the neurobiologists. But it does so at the cost of telling us to concede that we ourselves are ineffectual, that we are futile abstract beings detached from all practical activity in the world.

We may well wonder how a supposedly scientific worldview has drifted into implying this kind of unwelcome consequence. And it is, I think, worthwhile to look back here for a moment and search out its intellectual roots.

3

TRANSCENDENT NUMBERS
PYTHAGORAS AND PLATO

ALL IS NUMBER – OR IS IT?

The profound respect for mathematics, and for physics as the earthly embodiment of mathematics, which so deeply moved Newton and his contemporaries, comes originally from Pythagoras of Samos, who first declared in the sixth century BCE that "All is number". This was a strikingly different proposal from those of other philosophers of the time who were also looking for a universal explanation. Thales and Anaximander, for instance, sought that explanation in physical elements such as water, air or earth, beginning from phenomena such as water's changing to ice or steam. And enquiries like these eventually gave rise to modern physical science.

But Pythagoras, who was the first great Greek mathematician, approached the problem from a quite different angle. The

DOI: 10.4324/9781003411710-4

kind of example from which he started was not the relation between ice and water but the timeless relation between musical notes and the length of the strings that produced them. He believed that such ratios underlay the whole cosmos. Accordingly, starting with these patterns, he moved into wider and wider mathematical investigations, studying increasingly complex problems along with a small band of chosen scholars whom he trained in these mathematical arts:

> The Pythagoreans were... the forerunners to modern physicists, for just as they were interested in the forms embedded in numbers, so too they were interested in finding mathematical forms embedded in the physical world. That Pythagoreanisn was a true protomathematical science is apparent in Pythagoras' famous discovery of numerical ratios underlying musical harmonies... [A] string twice as long as another produces the same note an octave lower... The Pythagoreans also experimented with varying the thickness and tension of strings and looked for numerical patterns in the sounds produced. Their discovery of mathematical ratios underlying the phenomena of sound tangibly demonstrated that mathematics was not only an abstract game but that it inhered in the physical world.
> *(Wertheim 1997: 30–31)*

These results seem very much like what we might expect from a research institute today but the enterprise that produced them was entirely different. The atmosphere of the work was intensely religious. The core group of mathematical researchers was surrounded by a congregation of supporters who lived in accordance with Pythagoras' principles, observing various taboos such as vegetarianism and behaving soberly and nonviolently. This whole way of life was aimed at releasing the soul, which is trapped in the body during our present life, to follow its proper course into the divine world of numbers that it will return to after our death.

This was a new kind of religion in Greece. It was, of course, a product of an epoch when similar proposals were being made elsewhere, for instance by Confucius and Lao Tzu in China, by Zoroaster in Persia and by Buddha in India. In all these places people were growing dissatisfied with the somewhat parochial, anthropomorphic gods who had satisfied their forebears and were seeking for a purer and more universal source of enlightenment.

Pythagoras, who had travelled in the East and studied these religions, followed this path eagerly. He did not attack the traditional Greek gods, but simply removed their human character by identifying them with the numbers on which the spiritual enterprise was to centre. These numbers, he explained, were themselves divine beings: spiritual entities that we should contemplate because they were the rulers and directors of the cosmos. He thus developed a meditative way of life in which, after purification by means of the everyday virtues, students could rise to an exalted concentration on the patterns of this mathematical overworld.

This is an impressive ambition but it has some disturbing consequences. As Margaret Wertheim comments:

In parallel with this rather beautiful mysticism was another agenda, for in freeing the psyche the Pythagoreans were also attempting to escape from *nature*... Pythagoras equated divinity with timeless stasis and immutability, qualities which cannot be found anywhere in nature. Indeed the whole point of the number-gods was that they were beyond nature, with its inherent transience and mortality... Pythagoras equated divinity with timeless stasis and immutability.

(Ibid.: 28, original emphasis)

Thus humans were called on to leave the transience of nature and move away, towards the stillness of eternity. In this way, after death they would be able to enjoy a pure communion with the timeless entities to which they were profoundly akin. At this point, however, there is surely something of a problem. How is it that human souls, which are essentially mobile creatures, responding constantly to changes in the world, are akin to these dignified, rock-like, unchanging ideals? What have these two kinds of being in common? How could they communicate? Plato did notice this problem in his late work, but he never resolved it.

The doctrine also had another alarming effect that has not, I think, been fully understood today. It produced a bias against women. Both nature and the earth itself were viewed as female and therefore bad. Numbers, too, had moral characteristics; for instance, one was good because it stood for the benign unity of everything. All other odd numbers were therefore good – and male – while even numbers were female and therefore bad. Pythagoreans regularly classed female qualities as evil and good ones as male.

This idea had a significant effect on later thinking because the influence of Pythagoreanism did not die with its founder. Its mathematical discoveries were taken into the wider tradition of learning, but as a religion it survived vigorously for some time. Indeed, after Christianity had become widely accepted, Pythagoreanism revived among people who found it a rational spiritual alternative to the rising tide of Christianity. Plainly it was a religion that people could live by. And throughout the days of the later Roman Empire it still continued to attract seekers of enlightenment.

Its most important disciple, however, was Plato, who, as is well known, centred his worldview on the Pythagorean contrast between the temporary, shifting things that we encounter on earth and the eternal verities of the ideal world, such as numbers. Earthly things, he said, are not entirely unreal, but they draw what little reality they have from participating in transcendent ideals. Essentially the real is the rational, and that can never be found on earth.

His favourite examples of this came from mathematics. The circles that we draw are, he said, not really circular, not perfect examples. However good our compasses may be, there are still irregularities. What circularity they have is drawn from their incomplete participation in the Circle itself, the ideal model that is laid up in the eternal world along with other models or Forms. Apart from these figures and numbers, the most impressive examples of these Forms are the virtues, such as Justice. This suggestion that Justice itself and Pi should be viewed as kindred ideal entities is a powerful one that has led to much useful thinking. It needs, however, to be handled with much more care than it has often received.

There is, of course, something wild about Plato's duplication of worlds. It leads into the kind of dualism we have just been complaining about. Yet he has surely hit on some real problems here. When we condemn the justice that is meted out in our courts and say that it is "not real justice", what do we mean? What would real justice be? And again, when we add seven to thirteen and come up with twenty, what objects are we talking about? We know that this twenty is not just twenty dots or twenty apples, so what is it?

We do seem here to deal in a somewhat mysterious ideal world. And some mathematicians, who readily call themselves Platonists, still think it important to insist that numbers are indeed somehow independent realities. Plato raises serious questions about the kind of objectivity that is possible for mathematics and – what is even more important – for ethics, questions that still need thinking about. But in order to be clear about them we need to identify plainly the still-active way of thinking that grew out of them and which can still reasonably be called Platonism. It combines:

- a special reverence for mathematical studies and for the human logical faculties that conduct them, leading to the belief that only these studies form the ideal human life, since they alone allow us to glimpse reality;
- alienation from the earth and all its creatures, which may mean only detachment but can easily amount to exploitation, contempt and horror; and
- distrust, sometimes amounting to hostility, towards the female element in life and the human affections that it stands for.

During the Middle Ages this whole strand of thought was somewhat eclipsed by other ideas: first by Christian thinking, and then by the revived influence of Aristotle and by the notions of "natural magic" that we have already mentioned. (Aristotle, who strongly defended the single world of common sense against this mystical dualism, has always provided the most appropriate answers to it and he does so again today.) Platonism, however, always remained active, and at the Renaissance it surfaced again, centrally through the work of yet another philosopher who, like Pythagoras and Plato, was himself a major mathematician – René Descartes. His worldview, a kind of rationalism that exalted consecutive reasoning of the kind used in mathematics as the central source of all our knowledge, provided an admirable platform for the further developments in physics that followed from Copernicus's discovery of the centrality of the sun. And, although it was not so appropriate for other, more empirical forms of thought, these drawbacks were not at first much noticed.

This rationalistic worldview formed the background to Newton's thought, and it was the message that the band of enthusiasts who formed the Royal Society aimed, above all, to spread abroad. A very interesting indication of the priority they gave it appears in the well-known remarks of the Royal Society's own in-house philosopher, John Locke, about the condition of culture in his day. Asking in what ways he might reasonably expect his own enquiries to be useful, he breaks out into something of a rhapsody about the current condition of letters:

> The commonwealth of learning, is not at this time without master-builders, whose mighty designs, in advancing the sciences, will leave lasting monuments to the admiration of posterity: But everyone must not hope to be a Boyle, or a Sydenham; and in an age which produces such masters, as the great Huygenius, and the incomparable Mr Newton, with some other of that strain; 'tis ambition enough to be employed as an under-labourer in clearing ground a little, and removing some of the rubbish that lies in the way to knowledge... Vague and insignificant forms of speech, and abuse of language, have so long passed for mysteries of science... that it will not be easy to persuade, either those who speak, or those who hear them, that they are but the covers of ignorance, and hindrance of true knowledge.
>
> *([1689] 1997: "Epistle to the Reader", 10–11)*

It is surely somewhat remarkable that a philosopher who looks round at the intellectual scene to find impressive figures should pick on four physicists and no philosophers at all, and still more so that he should then claim to serve them as an under-labourer. This, after all, was an age in which the philosophical scene too was certainly not without its master-builders, for instance Leibniz and Spinoza. But these were full-time rationalists, opponents of the empiricist creed to which Locke was officially devoted, theorists whom he considered as particularly guilty of using the "vague and insignificant forms of speech" that he was so eager to tidy away.

Locke writes, very much in the style of recent therapeutic positivists, as if it was only the *language* of current philosophy that needed clearing up and no real problems underlay it. But in fact the gross problems about dualism that we have been mentioning lay all around him, and behind them was a further layer of difficulties about reconciling the patterns of his Cartesian rationalism with his alleged empiricist campaign.

CHRISTIAN PYTHAGOREANISM

The main reason why Locke and his friends did not notice these knots in their worldview is, I think, that they were thrown into shadow by the solid bulk of Anglican Christianity, which, as we have noticed, remained always a safe bulwark for the sages of the Royal Society. Christian thinking had always held an element of distaste for the earth, and the Pythagorean land of divine numbers was readily slotted into the Christian heaven. Wertheim comments:

> The central axis of Pythagorean mysticism – mathematics, maleness, and psychic transcendence – has also had a profound impact on the culture of Western physics. Because mathematics was seen as the study of the transcendent world of the gods, so too the quest for mathematical relationships in the physical world also came to be seen as a transcendent activity – a quest for that part of nature that was eternal, immutable, and incorruptible. When, in the Middle Ages, a Pythagorean spirit reemerged within the context of Christianity, this attitude was readily transformed into an association

between nature's mathematical relations and the Christian God. Like the ancient Pythagoreans, medieval and early modern physicists believed they were discovering a transcendent, deity-driven blueprint for creation.

(1997: 30)

What is surely remarkable, however, is that today, when scientists claim to have eliminated God, thus getting rid of any religion that could possibly make them believe in an afterlife, and when they are currently trying to get rid of the soul itself, this essentially Pythagorean attitude still seems to be so influential. Newton, Bacon and the founders of the Royal Society are still celebrated and acknowledged as the sources of today's attitude to science even though God, the central hinge of their system, is gone.

If we wonder why today's scientists are satisfied with this, I think a part of the answer surely is that, at heart, their ideas are – as Newton's were – still Pythagorean. That profoundly reverent attitude to mathematics itself – that conviction that basically all is number – has, it seems, been able to survive its divorce from Christianity, with which it had only a marriage of convenience. It continues as a religion on its own and we shall observe some more of its effect, especially in producing misogyny, in Chapters 10 and 12.

4

WHAT EXPLANATION IS

WHAT IS EXPLAINING?

To return to the present day, there are many points at which we could dive into the cheerful store of dilemmas that Crick and his colleagues provide for us, and we shall find that many different doctrines are involved. But perhaps as good a starting-point as any is to accept gratefully what we are being given: to attend first to the attractive promise that brain cells alone will now be able to explain all our thoughts and feelings.

How will they do this? In the recent spate of enthusiasm for neuroscience, such offers have frequently been made:

> The sociologist Scott Vrecko has listed neurobiological accounts of (take a deep breath) in alphabetical order: altruism, borderline personality disorder, criminal behaviour, decisionmaking, empathy, fear, gut feelings, hope, impulsivity,

DOI: 10.4324/9781003411710-5

judgement, love... , motivation, neuroticism, problem gambling, racial bias, suicide, trust, wisdom and zeal (religious).

(Tallis 2011: 73, citing Vrecko 2010)

"Knowledge of the mechanisms of the brain", Jeste said in an interview, "could potentially lead to developing interventions for enhancing wisdom".

(Ibid.: 75)

So what is being offered here? Usually, research has shown that a particular area of the brain lights up when its owner is apparently in the state of mind in question. There are, of course, some questions about the kind of reliability that can be expected from even the most sophisticated modern methods of scanning the brain. Raymond Tallis, after an appreciative description of these devices, makes this comment on their limitations:

The first thing to remember when you come across headlines such as "Found: The Brain's Centre of Wisdom" is that fMRI scanning doesn't directly tap into brain activity... (but) registers it only indirectly by detecting the increases in blood flow... Many *millions* of neurons have to be activated for a change in blood flow to be detected... All that can be observed [about the brain's reaction to a particular stimulus] is the *additional* activity associated with the stimulus... [which] can be identified only by a process of averaging the results of subtractions after the stimulus has been given repeatedly; variations in the response to successive stimuli are ironed out. The raw data tell a very different story from the cooked.

(Ibid.: 76–7, original emphasis)

From another angle, Roger Carpenter, Professor of Oculomotor Physiology at the University of Cambridge, complains that the dramatic appeal of today's colourful imagery constantly distracts researchers, as well as the public, from following up the serious questions. Altogether, he says:

> the phrenological way of looking at the brain – for example identifying the area for fear, or the area for doing up one's shoelaces – embodies a simplistic approach long abandoned in genetics... *Where is not how;* what we really need to know are not the locations of brain activity but the underlying neural mechanisms.
>
> *(Carpenter 2013: 32, emphasis added)*

But, provided that these difficulties could be overcome and the state of mind could be well identified – which is not easy to ensure – what would this process do? It would "explain" the thought in the same modest sense in which a car's engine explains its movements, namely, that the engine must be present and in good order for the car to move.

This doesn't, however, make the engine a sole cause of the movement. If you see a strange car driving into your garden, you do not only want to know how the engine works – you want to know what is intended. Cars need many other things just as badly as engines, for instance petrol, roads and a driver who knows where he is going. In the same way, a human mind needs the rest of its body, suitable surroundings and a full memory of past activities if it is to think and act. And it needs them every bit as badly as it needs its brain.

It is not clear, then, how a brain could "alone account for all our actions" or how any given part of it could alone account for some particular activity. This is why, even though neurology is of enormous use for medical purposes when the brain works badly, claims to use it to explain mental phenomena in healthy people are of very limited use. The news that a certain brain process is associated with a certain thought or feeling does not necessarily tell us anything new about that thought or feeling, anything that we did not already know more directly from subjective and social sources.

For instance, we did not have to wait for the discovery of mirror neurons in order to know that humans – and many other creatures too – can directly detect each other's feelings. All human interactions make it clear that our strong expressive capacity often enables us to perceive each other's feelings accurately without using language. This fact has certainly been known for as long as people have been communicating at all; indeed, it is notorious that this is just what makes deception so difficult. And, if authority were needed for this fact, Darwin himself took the trouble to write a whole and very impressive book about it – *On The Expression of the Emotions in Men and Animals* – a book that has not received half the attention it ought to have had in the recent centenary celebrations.

Yet the discovery of the cerebral machinery through which this expression works – mirror neurons – was greeted with as much astonishment as if it had revealed the performance itself. Indeed, it began to seem as if people had so far managed to ignore the evidence of their own experience about social interaction until official scientific notification forced them to recognize it. This is a striking example of two current strange assumptions: first, the assumption that we are originally quite separate from each other (which I have discussed elsewhere, in *The Solitary Self*); and, second, the assumption that the direct deliverances of our own experience are worthless until they have received official scientific authorization. This last idea is a central part of our business here.

That detached attitude to subjectivity limits the usefulness of many, perhaps of most, current offers to explain social and mental facts through observations from neuroscience. But fortunately the enterprise of understanding the effect of the two brain hemispheres on our lives is an exception. Something of great interest is emerging there. It turns out that the two halves of our brain play slightly different roles in forming our thoughts, the left one concentrating on discovering the details while the right attends to the wider picture. People whose right brain has been injured can still show many detailed skills, especially in speech, but they are unable to understand their wider situation.

Thus in normal life the two halves need to work together, but the extent to which they can do so depends on how we direct our attention. If the left brain is getting too much of that attention – if the right brain is not being consulted from time to time – then their owner cannot easily perceive that imbalance because the left brain itself is only able to notice details. Thus that eager scholar Pliny the Elder insisted on pursuing his researches into the eruption of Vesuvius to the point where he unfortunately got himself killed. And thus, particularly in the modern world, where many people make their living by detailed technical skills that depend on the left brain, it is extremely easy for wider, but absolutely vital, matters – for instance, climate change – to be entirely neglected. This is a really important matter that is now beginning to be much better understood than it once was. We shall discuss it more fully in Chapter 11.

This exception brings out another crucial point about the meaning of *explanation*. When we say that one thing explains or accounts for another we don't usually mean that it is the sole cause. We mean that it fills a crucial gap in our current explanatory scheme. If, for instance, you are trying to account for a particular tree you can certainly get some of your explanation by standard scientific methods: by taking it to pieces and perhaps eventually burning it. But if you know nothing about trees to start with this is not going to get you very far. You obviously need, for a start, a clear general idea about the nature of plants – more particularly information about trees and about this particular kind of tree – and, more particularly still, information about its life-history just where it grows, and the other life forms that have been active around it.

For instance, it may sustain all manner of small inhabitants. It may have been planted in a churchyard because it is a yew, and may have had its branches damaged because little boys have climbed on it. Questions can arise about endless aspects of the matter, and *the kind of explanation that we need depends entirely on which of these questions we think important at the time.* If, instead of a tree, we ask about some aspect of human life, the number of possible questions multiplies almost beyond imagination. The serious business of thought depends crucially on our skill in sorting out these questions.

OBJECTS NEED SUBJECTS

The idea of a sole cause for thought has, however, been so confidently proposed lately that it seems important to pause here and understand why it can't work. Consider how this confluence of causes functions in a particular case. For example, when Einstein – or Crick – tries out a new approach to a problem, he does indeed need to have his brain in good order so that he can use it. But he needs just as badly to have *in his mind* the whole background that has made his previous calculations possible. And he needs to go on attending sharply to the work of continuing it, for which purpose he must obviously remain conscious.

Thus, however surprising this may be, *it is an objective fact in the world that our own experiences – the subjective sources of thought – are every bit as necessary for it as the objective ones such as brain cells.* Your mind is not an optional spare part; it is you, considered as a thinker, feeler and chooser rather than just as a physical object. At least, that is how things are in this present life that we have to live now. If they will be different after death we shall have to deal with that new problem when it arises.

Subjectivity, then, is not an irrelevance, not a shameful secret; it is the basic stuff of experience. Experience is what we start from and what every demand for verification must come back to. And since *empiricism* itself just means "belief in experience" empiricists are supposed to take this first-person activity seriously. Thought starts in that first person and proceeds to the second before it ever gets to the third, which is the home of objects and objectivity.

That is why Einstein cannot simply lie back and let the cells do the job for him. As we know, he must do the work himself, moved by his own joys and sorrows, his own memories and ambitions, his own sense of personal identity and free will. If these were not real, thought would stop. Any disturbance that blocks his memory or attention will end the calculation in its tracks, no matter how many brain cells are still waiting to continue it. Although a great deal of background thinking goes on beneath the conscious surface – for instance during sleep – this support is likely to fail if active concentration does not return to work on it. And the cognitive background that may be relevant here is enormous. It includes not just the current state of physics and the whole cultural context that produced it but also a personal lifetime of other experience and other thinking. All those past happenings equally are among the sources of his present thinking.

Thought, in fact, is not an isolated performance by a few neurons isolated in a single brain. It is part of a huge network that is continuous with the vast world that is its subject matter. The roots and tendrils of thought are everywhere. It is pervasive because it is not, as dualists have supposed, a supernatural alien substance intruded into our physical existence but an organic element of life, an activity as natural to us as seeing or eating. As Lynn Margulis puts it:

> The mind and the body are not separate but part of the unified process of life. Life, sensitive from the onset, is capable of thinking.... Thought, like life, is matter and energy in flux; the body is its "other side". Thinking and being are the same thing.
>
> *(1995: 188)*

Thus the necessary conditions for thought can never be simple. They radiate out indefinitely in a hundred directions and there is room for all of them. Mental causes do not block or compete with physical causes. Both are needed and all are equally real. So there cannot be such a thing as a sole cause or a sole explanation.

CAN THE BRAIN TAKE CHARGE?

How much each of these influences actually affects our thoughts and actions we can know only from experience. Recent advances in neuroscience, and in the imagery that dramatizes it, have certainly proved useful for various medical purposes. Indeed, studying the mind via the brain does seem to be most helpful when that brain is going wrong. But how helpful this approach will turn out to be over the whole range of social and psychological topics just listed – how much relevant explanation it will give us for the questions that actually puzzle us – is still quite uncertain. Not many striking revelations of this kind seem to have emerged so far.

And on the one central point that emerges from the car analogy – the extent to which brain cells can replace drivers as well as engines – mystery still reigns. In spite of much serious work by sciencefiction writers there are no reports so far of intelligent real-life activities performed solely by neurons without consciousness. Zombies are a thin myth without useful consequences.

In enquiries about all this the brain now often figures, as the gene did a little time ago, as an independent impresario, a substitute agent organizing things, a manager brought in by people who want to account somehow for purposive activities without involving ordinary human agents. At various times other theorists have invoked various other substitute agents to work their various forms of determinism: behaviour patterns, economic trends, historical forces, evolution, the class system. And there has often been some truth in these suggestions. The trouble is that none of these things can be the sole cause because there are always a dozen others at work. The kind of determinism that theorists dream of here – a prefixed pattern that would ensure reliable prediction – could only really work within a closed system. And no such systems are available.

It is already clear, then, that we cannot simply settle the mind–body problem right away, as these sages propose, by dropping the mind and handing its work over to the neurons. Much of that work is beyond them. The kinds of explanation needed for serious human problems are complicated and must come from both sides. If a chess game is going on, the latest move needs to be explained in terms of chess as well as in terms of neurology and the laws of gravitation that affect the pieces on the board.

So we have no alternative here but to rethink our whole situation. We need to look freshly at this strange pair – mind and body – and to see how odd our notions about them have become. Ought they ever to have been divided in the first place?

HOLLOW MATERIALISM

Current opinions display a curious contradiction here. Officially, scientifically minded people today are strict materialists. They are sure that only matter is real. But since almost every topic that comes before them is shot through with human plans and intentions, in practice they are still dualists, living in a world made of two apparently disconnected kinds of stuff.

Thus, if they are called on to deal with some non-material force – for instance with money, or curiosity, or bad temper, or nationalism, or logic, or market forces, or the law – they do not just complain that this force is unreal. Nor do they insist on translating it into the movements of neurons or, indeed, of quarks. They ask no awkward questions. They simply treat it as real – that is, as effective. Or again, if someone asks them a question about some problem that really interests them they do not usually just refuse to think about it on the grounds that this thinking will be useless because their thoughts can never affect the world.

What this shows is that their professed exclusive materialism is not serious. It is a convention that is supposed to apply only to selected areas of life. Inside those areas it is accepted as scientific currency, rather like the special Musical Bank money that respectable citizens of Erewhon were so careful to be seen handling: an intellectual coinage necessary for appearances, but no use for spending. Colourful conventions like this often persist, protecting idle doctrines, delaying changes that will finally have to be made and making people feel that those changes can never come. They harden cognitive dissonance. They institutionalize humbug, in this case, pseudo-scientific humbug which is a crucial element in the myths that rule us today.

5

WHY THE IDEA OF PURPOSE WON'T GO AWAY

FUNCTIONS, TASTES AND LIKINGS

A very interesting example of this rather airy theorizing is the belief that teleology – reasoning from purpose – has been cut out from scientific thought. One of the first lessons that biology students now learn is that they must never argue teleologically – never ask about purpose because purpose has no place in nature. Yet in explaining any piece of behaviour, human or otherwise, researchers regularly proceed by looking for its evolutionary function. The reasoning that is needed to discover this function is in fact of exactly the kind that has long been used to seek out the aims of any process. The questioner simply asks: what's it for? The only new feature is that now only one answer will be allowed. The function of anything organic

DOI: 10.4324/9781003411710-6

must be self-perpetuation: the tendency of the behaviour to enhance the behaving individual's reproductive prospects.

Whether or not this way of looking at things makes it easier to understand evolution, it certainly does not get rid of teleology. What it prescribes is a very simple teleology that allows only a single aim for all development. This strategy certainly changes the imaginative drama of life as we see it. Studied in this way, life appears much less spontaneous and more mechanical than it did before. The individual organisms that might seem to be its subjects – creatures with needs, tendencies and directions of their own – have evaporated, leaving a world of pure objects, fated for some reason to proceed in a way that will make them continually reproduce themselves. Noticing the oddity of this, Brian Goodwin remarked:

> All theories carry with them a particular viewpoint, a way of seeing phenomena that produces sharp focus on certain aspects of reality and blurred vision elsewhere. A striking paradox that has emerged from Darwin's way of approaching biological questions is that organisms, which he took to be primary examples of living nature, have faded away to the point where they no longer exist as fundamental and irreducible units of life. Organisms have been replaced by genes and their products as the basic elements of biological reality.... [Instead, organisms are now seen as] complex molecular machines controlled by the genes carried within them ...
>
> ... They have succumbed to the onslaught of an overwhelming molecular reductionism.
>
> *(Goodwin 1995: ix–x)*

This apparent personification of the genes is, of course, just a metaphor, but – since it still implies a purpose – it is one that seems bound to leave us still asking questions about what all this activity is for, still wanting to find the meaning of the behaviour of living things (including humans). But the natural, direct way to do this is surely to treat these individuals seriously, not as objects but as *subjects*, creatures with needs, tendencies and directions of their own. The idea that the world consists of objects without any such subjects does not really make sense at all.

Let us start our enquiry by asking: what is an evolutionary function and how does it work?

I noticed how confused current views about this are when I read a piece in the *Guardian* newspaper (Barkham 2010) about how entomologists hunt the impressive Purple Emperor butterfly. Apparently they must lay out its favourite diet, which is chiefly carrion and various kinds of faeces. Patrick Barkham says that Victorian observers were distressed by these tastes in such a noble animal and: "observed these degraded moments with a morbid fascination. *For the emperor, it is not, however, a question of taste.* It is thought that the males replenish themselves after mating, with sodium and other chemicals from the rotting matter" (*ibid.*: 6, emphasis added).

Thus we see the conscientious butterfly holding its proboscis and sternly taking its nasty medicine to protect its dynastic future. And this is the sort of picture that constantly emerges from contemporary evolution-talk: a picture that mixes two quite different kinds of purpose. The butterfly's own subjective purpose concerns what it wants to do. But the possible effect on the survival of its species is an evolutionary function, of which the butterfly knows nothing.

It is not surprising that these two ideas get mixed today. Official scientific thought doesn't now try to distinguish between different forms of purpose; indeed, it hardly recognizes the concept of purpose at all. Subjective purposes – motives – were outlawed from science-speak by the behaviourists, along with the rest of our inner life. Although their effects are obviously real, these purposes were blotted out so successfully from the perception of the learned that many conscientious thinkers still don't dare to look at them. Instead, in a way that would have delighted B. F. Skinner, they still try to account for physical actions directly in physical terms. They pick out distinct behaviour patterns and try to link each to an evolutionary function of its own, without reference to its meaning or its social context.

A recent controversy about the origins of nose-picking in humans showed the oddity of this. Since this habit is common, scientists suggested an amazing number of arcane physical mechanisms by which it might have directly improved people's breathing and thus their survival prospects. What nobody did was to ask about this habit's relation to *motives*, for instance to curiosity, to our tendency to explore and investigate things.

Like other primates we like to pry into mysterious places such as holes and this interest surely has affected our species survival in many ways, both helpful and otherwise. The details of the endless acts that it produces don't matter; what affects survival is the general interest. Human behaviour is not a ragbag of modules, disconnected behaviour patterns with separate evolutionary histories. *What evolves is an emotional constitution that shapes our lives as a whole*. We have to explain particular actions by finding their place in this constitution.

Thus, when we want to understand a real person's action we always start by looking for the motivational context. We try to spot the particular reason for the act and then to place it on our general map of motivation, a map that we must all use as we try to find our way through everyday life. We ask, was that clumsy remark just a misplaced effort to be helpful? Did it express resentment? Was it even part of a spiteful scheme to make trouble? Or perhaps a bit of all three?

It is, of course, fearfully confused to dismiss this interest in subjective matters as being somehow culpably subjective itself. It is not a fantasy, not just "folk-psychology", not a crude, amateur substitute for scientific investigation, but a necessary factual enquiry. It is the only way we can start to make sense of the life that goes on around us. Of course it's fallible, but on the whole it works and its success is one of the things that science needs to investigate. Evolutionary considerations are no substitute for it.

THE MOTIVATIONAL BACKGROUND

Another interesting case concerns something more important than nose-picking: the origin of speech. Michael Gazzaniga considers the following problem, which was raised by the evolutionary psychologist Geoffrey Miller:

> Most speech appears to transfer useful information from the speaker to the listener, and it costs time and energy. It seems to be altruistic. What fitness benefit can be attained by giving another individual good information? Reviewing the original argument of Richard Dawkins and John Krebs, Miller states, "Evolution cannot favor altruistic information-sharing any more than it can favor altruistic food-sharing. Therefore, most animals' signals must have evolved to manipulate the behavior of another animal for the signaller's own benefit". And other animals have evolved to ignore them, because it didn't pay to benefit the manipulators.
>
> *(Gazzaniga 2008: 107–8, quoting Miller 2001: 347)*

Miller asks how it can be that our species has managed to buck this trend by actually developing speech. His conclusion is (says Gazzaniga) that "language's complexities evolved for verbal courtship. This solves the altruism problem by providing a sexual payoff for eloquent speaking by the male and the female" (2008: 109).

Marilynne Robinson, who quotes this jewel of speculation in her splendid book *Absence of Mind* (Robinson 2010: 45–6), points out how odd it is to credit *courtship* with having played such a crucial role in the history of our species, when we know that the tradition of human societies is to treat marriages as strictly family business, dealt with by the elders, not by the parties concerned. More centrally, too, she remarks on the wildness of this approach in which "our nature is defined as if determined by the nature of hypothetical primitives, human-like in their ability to have and give information, *but finding neither use nor pleasure in doing so*" (ibid.: 45, emphasis added).

The trouble is that theorists who think natural selection can only work by cut-throat competition between individuals pursue that pattern obsessively, without glancing at the social phenomena they are supposed to be explaining. Thus, Miller does not seem to have noticed that speech does not just convey separate bytes of information, to be carried home and secretly devoured in one's lair. Speech, along with the rest of communication, is a vital medium, an ambient ocean in which we all swim, a power that allows us to make a whole mass of essential social moves. As Wittgenstein remarked, we do not use it just for informing but for all kinds of interactions that are vital to our lives – "asking, thanking, cursing, greeting, praying" (Wittgenstein 1951: part 1, §23). Although these scholars presumably know, like the rest of us, that a direct wish for a special sort of interaction with other people constantly determines how we act, they still believe that, behind this screen, there must lie hidden the real causes, elements of evolutionary advantage private to ourselves. However hard that advantage may be to find – however little possibility there may be that any evidence could reveal it – it is still the real McCoy.

Thus the real point and value of life is held to lie in its producing more life – life that will exist only in order to repeat the process, much like those unlucky people who only know how to make money and never learn how to spend it. This strange kind of teleology allows only one aim. Niles Eldredge asks, in his admirable book about the meaning of sex, *Why We Do It: Rethinking Sex and the Selfish Gene* "How reasonable an assumption can it be that we eat to live, but live to reproduce...? We cannot have sex without living, yet we can live without having sex" (2004: 32). And in fact living itself provides us with plenty of reasons to go on doing it. We live mainly for the present, not the future.

Sociobiology's preference for supposed occult dynastic motives over obvious social ones is not a parsimonious way of thinking and neither, as it happens, is it Darwinian. In *The Descent of Man*, Darwin argued strongly that we are not just a sociable species but are naturally more sociable – more cooperative, affectionate and interdependent – than any of our relatives. Our social instincts are, he said, so crucial to our lives that they must have been strongly developed during evolution by means of group selection: by the differential survival of coherent, friendly groups over less interactive ones. These instincts therefore now ground our motives and shape the complexity of our lives. So the idea of deriving all our motivation from the single stem of selfishness, or enlightened self-interest, is (said Darwin) radically mistaken.

6

IS SEXUAL SELECTION
NATURAL?

ATOMISTIC GENETICS

During the mid-twentieth century, Darwin's suggestion that
group-selection was the source of our sociability was, of course,
suppressed because this form of selection was then believed to
be impossible. At that time, evolutionists made selection at only
one level into a compulsory orthodoxy. Rationality demanded
(it seemed) that competition should take place only between
a single set of rivals: evolutionary atoms that profited individ-
ually from the process. These units, which at first had seemed
to be whole organisms, were finally deemed to be the genes
and were treated as independent agents in a way that seemed to
credit them with having purposes of their own. The imagery of
"selfishness", which expressed the supposed isolation and eager
activity of these rivals, was seen as crucial for the process.

DOI: 10.4324/9781003411710-7

The resulting mythology of egoism suited the Thatcherite age so well that the story seemed, for a while, convincing to many scientists as well as to the public. Later, however, serious cracks began to appear in it, not least because it was clear that genes themselves are not actually individualists but highly co-operative. It emerged that the simple atomistic pattern was not workable nor necessary, that natural selection can perfectly well go on at a number of different levels between units of different kinds. As David Sloan Wilson put it:

> The past half-century was the age of reductionism, when everything was explained in terms of individual self-interest and selfish genes. Now we are entering the age of holism which recognises how colonies of social insects, human societies and at least some multispecies ecosystems can respond as a single "superorganism" to selective pressures.
>
> The turning-point came in the 1970s, when biologist Lynn Margulis proposed that complex, nucleated cells originated as symbiotic associations of bacterial cells. Now it is known that every entity recognised as an organism is a highly organised group of individual cells, making it hard to deny that groups of organisms can themselves have organism-like properties and so can evolve in concert.
>
> *(2010: 34)*

Similarly, Edward O. Wilson, whose book *Sociobiology: The New Synthesis* (1975) was a key text of the individualistic doctrine, has now moved away from it and thinks other patterns, such as group selection, can give better explanations even for the social insects that are his speciality and which were viewed for a time as prime examples of gene selection.

David Sloan Wilson (2008) also points out that group selection is particularly plausible in the case of humans because of the invention of speech. A group that can talk is able to pass round, and to profit from, any new invention much, much faster than any new developments could ever be spread genetically. In this way a new hunting method, a new cooking pot, a new family structure or a new style of government can quickly profit a human group that is cooperative enough to produce it, making these people more successful than their neighbours who don't bother to talk to one another. Speech, in fact, does have its evolutionary advantages, but only for groups of people who like each other enough to attend to their neighbours.

HOW NATURAL IS SEXUAL SELECTION?

Yet another interesting case of confusion about evolutionary function concerns Darwin's discussion of sexual selection: the choosing of mates and its effect on the progeny. He added this long, separate section to his book *The Descent of Man* because he clearly saw it as an important supplement to his general account of natural selection. But the name he gave it seems odd. In the text he repeatedly contrasts *sexual* selection with *natural* selection as if it were something unnatural. What he seems to mean is that ordinary, standard "natural selection" is the kind that works simply by differential dying: by one kind of variant being lost in greater numbers than another.

He did, of course, believe that this was the main source of evolutionary change, and it was the only source that he talked about in *The Origin of Species*. But he was always sure that it was not the only source, and he got quite cross when people claimed he thought it *was* the only one.

No doubt this was because he could see that this explanation alone could not possibly be adequate. *Selection by differential survival is only a filter, and filters have no originative force. They do not create the novelty, the coffee that flows out of them.* New, positive kinds of development need their own source.

This was surely why Darwin always remained interested in Lamarck's suggestion that acquired characteristics were somehow inherited, even though he could not see how. And it is something that we badly need to take notice of today, because it knocks the bottom out of our current idea that natural selection is the only force behind evolution. The range of candidates that are present for "selection" to select from – the spectrum of possibilities that might prevail – have to come from somewhere else, and that somewhere has to be the innate creative capacities of matter. About these capacities we know very little, and we are certainly not going to learn more from physics.

Besides this metaphorical kind of selection by death, Darwin saw also a different kind that visibly went on in the world around him: the process by which creatures actually choose their mates – literal choice rather than the figurative kind. (The awkward effects of the selection metaphor have, of course, often been noticed, but I don't think people have grasped quite how badly that metaphor obscures the word's literal meaning.) Darwin had watched how animals make their choices and had seen its striking effects in the decorations that so many of them wear, especially animals with a strong visual interest, such as birds and insects. He saw that these ornaments often seemed to have no other function than this and that some of them appeared only during mating displays. So he documented their effectiveness and illustrated it with careful drawings.

WHOSE ARTISTRY?

His readers, however, did not readily believe him. Scientists found it absurd to suggest that something so trifling and capricious as the taste of individual birds – especially female birds – could have such momentous effects. They agreed that the ornaments in question were indeed amazingly, unaccountably subtle and beautiful. But this only made them even less able to believe that mere animals could ever have appreciated them. Repeatedly, Darwin showed his reasoning about this:

The case of the male Argus pheasant is eminently interesting, because it affords good evidence that the most refined beauty may serve as a charm for the female, *and for no other purpose.* We must conclude that this is the case, as the primary wing-feathers are never displayed, and the ball-and-socket ornaments are not seen in their full perfection, except when the male assumes the attitude of courtship.... Many will declare that it is *utterly incredible that a female bird should be able to appreciate fine shading and exquisite patterns.* It is undoubtedly a marvellous fact that she should possess *this almost human degree of taste*, though perhaps she admires the general effect rather than each separate detail. *He who thinks that he can safely gauge the discrimination and taste of the lower animals,* may deny that the female Argus pheasant can appreciate such refined beauty; but he will then be compelled to admit that the extraordinary attitudes assumed by the male during the act of courtship, by which the wonderful beauty of his feathers is fully displayed, are purposeless; and this is a conclusion which I for one will never admit.

([1871] 1981: 92–3, emphasis added)

What was obvious to him, but apparently quite invisible to his critics, was that human tastes too arise out of our nature as animals. (Similarly, we might notice that the Purple Emperor isn't the only creature that eats its meat high, or that has a taste for salt.) Darwin touched on this delicate issue when he discussed the various features in animals that appear to work as ornaments for them, although they don't strike us as beautiful. He writes:

> No certain answer can be given to these questions; but we ought to be cautious in assuming that knobs and various fleshy appendages cannot be attractive to the female, when we remember that with savage races of man various hideous deformities – deep scars on the face with the flesh raised into protuberances, the septum of the nose pierced by sticks and bones, holes in the ears and lips stretched widely open – are all admired as ornamental.
>
> *(Ibid.: 129–30)*

Even human observers, in fact, don't always have faultless taste or one that agrees with our own. Their preferences differ from culture to culture. We do find, however, that people in different cultures commonly share some basic aesthetic judgements. And, as it happens, one of the points on which different societies most readily agree is a widespread admiration for the elegant plumes of birds, which are sought out and used as ornaments in a great range of cultures.

Who, however, designed these wonderful feathers? Certainly not a human. If Darwin is right, the artists here seem to have been the birds themselves, which means (since the males usually have the best feathers) chiefly their wives. So is there not something oddly condescending about scientists presuming to doubt whether these original designers are themselves capable of the "almost human degree of taste" that would be needed to appreciate their work?

KEEPING THINGS QUIET

There were, I think, two reasons why Darwin's critics found these suggestions so disturbing. One, of course, was simply the species barrier: the habit of considering humans as so remote from other animals that it became almost impossible to imagine any continuity between them, even when argument showed this to be necessary. This was, of course, always a main source of difficulty about accepting Darwinian reasoning, which was far more directly offensive to notions of human dignity than to the status of God. But another obstacle here is just as strong but perhaps less obvious, namely unwillingness to take seriously the influence of subjective happenings on the world.

Darwin was suggesting that the wishes of hen-pheasants – their inner thoughts and feelings as they watched their various suitors – had affected, and had finally determined, the design of later generations. This thought is frightening when it concerns animals but even more when it concerns people. The difficulty is quite general.

Of course it is never easy to accept the role that the thoughts and feelings of our own parents – and indeed of other people's – on similar occasions have played in making things be as they are now. Yet we know that these thoughts and feelings, not only then but throughout their lives, have indeed had this sort of importance. Our own thoughts and feelings too – the constant flow of inner activity by which we respond to the life around us – also affect the world as well as our outward actions. This thought is so frightening that scholars will often go to any lengths to avoid it, which is why T. H. Huxley's obviously mistaken epiphenomenalist doctrine that our thoughts do not affect our actions still has supporters (a matter we shall discuss in Chapter 12).

That is why people spend so much more of their time on sociological statistics, neurological details and speculation about evolutionary function than they do on attending to urgent problems about motive. This inhibition on talk of subjectivity has got a lot worse since the behaviourist campaign that forced psychologists to regard the inner life as an indecent topic. A hundred years ago, William James, Freud and their contemporaries readily explored difficult problems about motivation, looking at both its conscious and its subconscious forms.

This often led to their demonstrating how hard these problems actually are, which may have been one reason why their colleagues were increasingly prone to ignore them. In particular, Freud – who asked good questions about important topics, although he didn't always give good answers – was seen (after Karl Popper denounced him in the 1950s) as inexcusably unscientific. And, although psychologists had in theory abandoned behaviourist doctrines, in practice they increasingly chose topics that the behaviourists would have approved of, topics that could easily be made external and quantitative.

This choice of topics is, of course, a central factor in determining the direction of research. I remember being struck, after the difference between short- and long-term memory began to be discussed some two or three decades ago, by the eager way in which psychologists piled in to work on this matter. One would have thought this was a central issue for understanding human conduct, instead of being just a moderately interesting subject that had the advantage of stirring no emotions. And the biologists who continued Darwin's investigations about evolution after his death were clearly moved by the same sort of preference for avoiding drama in their choice of topics. They ignored the enquiries that he had begun to make about instinctive behaviour and the expression of emotion and concentrated instead purely on selection for survival.

LIFE HAS MANY COLOURS

That is why the picture of natural selection that grew up around Darwin's main proposals used only two sombre colours: black for death and white for survival. Nature appeared in it only as an obsessive accountant, spectacles on nose and ledger in hand, testing every action in those terms and destroying the failures. Any trait still appearing in the world was deemed to have passed her audit in some distinct, discoverable way that constituted its evolutionary function.

This figure of Nature is, of course, quite unlike the sort of nature we actually find at work in the animal and vegetable world, where it is notoriously a cornucopia, a wildly lavish scatterer of endless seeds and young, a generous, profuse, imprudent source of new life. And when we consider our own motives, we see that this vegetatious figure is a far better likeness of the kind of nature that animates us inwardly. Life for us is not just the absence of death. Life consists of endless crowded, positive wishes, fears and activities, all primed by their own immediate aims and interests, not by long-term prudence. Like other conscious creatures we usually take action because we want to, and if our nature did not provide us with many vigorous wants we could not act at all.

Of course, it is true that if a particular innate taste, such as a taste for eating toadstools, has fatal consequences it will tend to be lost from the species's repertoire. But, in all kinds of animals, a huge number of wishes have no particular effect at that level and work only for the general enrichment of life. No one who watches seagulls swooping and rising is likely to see reason to think that they are only taking the exact amount of exercise they need to keep their constitution in optimal health. And the same goes for human children.

It seems perfectly possible, too, that some tastes persist, even though they actually harm survival prospects, because other characteristics outweigh this damage. After all, even the human physique has notorious imperfections, such as the bad design of our throats, where food and breath get into dangerous

competition. Similarly, the splendid tails of peacocks are notoriously awkward for their flight, yet peacocks are still with us.
This is surely a grave objection to the socio-biological insist-
ence that everything has an evolutionary function.

Helena Cronin (1991) produced an ingenious defence
against this attack, suggesting that the defect really acts as an
advertisement, letting the hen know that this must be a particularly powerful male since he has been able to get away with
carrying such a dangerous burden. In this way, of course, it is
possible to count any given drawback as an asset, thereby saving
the principle that every characteristic has a survival function.
But this way of saving principles by turning them into matters
of logic has the unlucky effect of leaving them without any real
meaning, something that, at one time, notoriously used to happen to Freudian principles. It is not an effective way of escape.

MOTIVES ARE REAL

One way or another, then, the attempt to find an evolutionary advantage in terms of survival for every human taste –
including, say, the taste for doing mathematics, for jokes and
laughter, for music and poetry, for play, for sympathizing or
for quarrelling – has proved perverse and empty. These are
things that are done for their own sake because they fulfil our
nature. The tendency at present is to connect them all with
evolution by claiming that they promote survival because they
are bond-forming. But the kind of bond formed in each case
is different and the effects on survival are infinitely varied.
This suggestion does nothing to explain the peculiar character
of these various occupations. To understand them, we need to
look at the distinctive part they each play in real life, not at
speculations about how they might possibly have prevented
some distant ancestor from dying.

Clearly, Darwin for one did not think this was the only way of explaining motives. He saw that there was more than one kind of question to be answered. As we saw, the case of the Argus pheasant shows, he says, that "the most refined beauty may serve as a charm for the female, *and for no other purpose*". Of course he was not denying that successful courtship as a whole serves another kind of purpose in its effect on the species. But he sees that the immediate point of these activities must lie in its meaning for the creatures that are acting. This subjective aspect is its central function.

He did not, then, invent a just-so story – as his supposed followers might do now – to make this fit neatly into his views on natural selection. Instead, he added a further long section to his work, dealing in detail with selection in its literal sense. He stuck to the actual cocks and hens involved and showed how these factors work in their lives. He openly talked of subjectivity and used words such as *charm* and *beauty* that are appropriate to it. Because this language embarrasses his successors they dismiss his suggestions as naive and old-fashioned. In their view all subjective phenomena are merely superficial appearances, perhaps actually illusions. The reality behind them is always an evolutionary function, which sounds reassuringly objective because the word *function* suggests machines.

But machines are certainly not value-free. They are indeed often thought of as *objective* because they are not people. But they are produced by people. They have always been designed by someone for some special purpose: to do some particular thing that their designers wanted done. So we cannot eliminate purpose from the natural world by describing it in terms of machines. The whole project of scientific positivism was, however, to eliminate all such wanting from descriptions of the world, thus producing pure statements of objective fact, undefiled by emotion. As we have seen, it was meant to produce a world of objects without subjects, which is really not an intelligible idea at all. The behaviourists' attempt to ignore motives was part of this vast and crazy enterprise, which is often celebrated by saying that teleology has become obsolete.

WIDER EVOLUTIONARY AMBITIONS

The word *teleology*, however, does not cover just conscious human purposes but the whole of function. Aristotle, who first worked out this form of explanation, never thought of it as arising from the purposes of a creative god, an idea quite alien to Greek thought. He used it simply for the kind of questioning that asks what particular things are *for*: what they do for the organism that owns them, what is their *telos*, their end or aim in the context where they belong. As he pointed out, this kind of reasoning is so indispensable in biology, and the aims it seeks are usually so obvious, that no other way of thinking can displace it. It is simply a fact that all organisms constantly strive towards their own survival, their health, their well being, their general fulfilment and their reproduction.

Thus an acorn placed under a paving-stone will not simply settle down contentedly to an underground existence. Instead it will do its damnedest to get out past that stone and to fulfil exactly the ambitions that are involved in being an oak tree. Human conscious purpose is not the prime model here. Human action is just one form of this universal striving, which is something far more pervasive in the world than our conscious kind of purpose. These are the only terms in which the behaviour of living things can be understood at all.

So should we then ask: does evolution itself also have its own purpose, its own guiding strategy? In theory, today's scientific thought excludes this idea. Indeed, officially it won't even countenance much smaller purposes. It holds that to say that legs are organs for walking is only to say that walking is what legs do. But this formula is so unhelpfully thin that people seldom try to follow it. The language of *adaptation* and *selection* proceeds quite naturally, as it always has done, by assuming familiar aims.

This habit is greatly helped by the word *evolution* itself, which has always carried the implication of a fixed direction. Like *development*, this word means the unrolling of something like a scroll or a bud, the fulfilment of a given potentiality. And the various evolutionary prophets have all had their views about what this pre-existing direction is. They usually state them in highly general terms that seem suited to so vast a process. But since they also want to say something useful for their readers' lives, they almost inevitably couch these generalities in local human terms.

They assume, for a start, that humanity itself is central to this cosmic aim, and then that whatever aspect of human life strikes them as primary constitutes the end of evolution. Thus Herbert Spencer defined the word as meaning "an integration of matter and concomitant dissipation of motion, during which the matter passes from an indefinite, incoherent homogeneity to a definite, coherent heterogeneity". From this he swiftly concluded that human individuality is the prime evolutionary value, and that therefore free trade is good and big government very dangerous. Enterprising individuals must be selectively encouraged and the feckless poor must be stopped from distorting evolution by breeding too freely.

Rather differently, Julian Huxley taught that a deep, scientifically guided reverence for the evolutionary process itself provides a kind of humanism that is the best modern substitute for religion. But his humanism too required eugenics, since it demanded that we civilized people – who are now, as he says, the growing-point of evolution – should control all human reproductive development and direct it rightly. Differently again, the cosmologists John Barrow and Frank Tipler took a more remote perspective, describing evolution as consisting in prolonged development of Life, which roughly = intelligence = science + technology. This Life, first in human form and then through a series of computerized cosmic probes that would colonize space, would finally, at the Omega Point, become omniscient and take over the universe, thus apparently becoming God (1986: 677; note the final footnote). And so on.

These suggestions have all, in their day, been put forward as scientific. None of them, however, is popular with scientists today. The Nazis discredited Spencer's and Huxley's eugenic ideas, while the cosmic alternative exists now mainly in science fiction. And there was another reason why these attempts to direct the evolutionary process were doomed. The total reliance of natural selection on chance was simply not compatible with the notion of any fixed direction. Conway Morris comments:

> As Julian's grandfather had dimly perceived, the naturalistic program would open the door to manipulation of a world from which meaning had fled. Thus the march "towards ever higher levels of order and value" [which Julian Huxley had posited] remained a chimaera.
>
> *(2003: 318)*

What officially prevails now among many scientists is the supposedly more economical view that the cosmos has no meaning at all – that, as Dawkins puts it, the universe contains, "at bottom, no design, no purpose, no evil and no good, nothing but blind, pitiless indifference" (1995: 155). That sounds value-free enough. But Dawkins, after writing "DNA neither cares nor knows. DNA just is", rather surprisingly goes on to write "And we dance to its music". His metaphor, like most metaphors, betrays the underlying intention. You can't produce music unless you have a purpose and are able to fulfil it. Dawkins's image can surely only mean that DNA does have a purpose, namely the vast cosmic purpose of maximizing all reproduction, which it is somehow in a position to impose on everything, including us. And it is false economy to take pride in making things unintelligible.

What we have here is, in fact, a form of fatalism. We are still in the same intensely teleological world that we heard about in Dawkins's book *The Selfish Gene*. We are still lumbering robots, helpless in the manipulating hands of these obsessively purposeful genes, which turn out (rather surprisingly) to be in charge not only of this planet but of the whole universe.

This lush mythology of gene-selfishness supplies the teleological jam that is always needed to make thin scientific stories like this go down. And the confident certainty of finding evolutionary functions for everything provides psychologists with a most flexible background for every speculation. In fact (as many people have pointed out) if you try to sling Nature – or indeed the whole idea of Nature – out through the door, she always comes quietly back down the chimney. And this may leave you even worse off than you were before. There is surely nothing to be said for fatalism.

7

THE SEARCH FOR SENSELESSNESS

It is no surprise that the pettiness of many proposed evolutionary purposes put orthodox biologists off teleology altogether;
they produced, in fact, an advanced case of teleophobia. And
even the slightly wider point that our own species is central
to evolution – a notion still potent with "human exceptional-
ists" today – has no clear scientific warrant. In fact, none of the
candidate ideas proposed as evolutionary purposes looks very
impressive.

That, however, certainly cannot mean that there is no such
thing as purpose in nature. Dawkins's claim that the universe
contains "at bottom, no design, no purpose, no evil and no
good" cannot be right. For it is obvious that our own planet –
which is certainly part of the universe – is riddled with purpose. It is full of organisms, beings that all steadily pursue their

DOI: 10.4324/9781003411710-8

own characteristic ways of life, beings that can be understood only by grasping the distinctive thing that each of them is trying to be and do. And as for *good* and *evil*, some quite definite things are good and others evil for each of them, because each has its own appropriate needs and capacities. Thus, being put under water is fine for fish but bad for zebras. And in human life too, despite cultural variety, experience has shown plenty of goods and evils that are naturally given and cannot be changed. The difficulty that we have is in choosing among these various values, not in inventing them. As Geoffrey Warnock pointed out, these are facts if anything is:

> We all have, and should not let ourselves be bullied out of, the conviction that at least some questions as to what is good and bad for people, what is harmful or beneficial, are not in any serious sense matters of opinion. That it is a bad thing to be tortured or starved, humiliated or hurt, is not an opinion, it is a fact. That it is better for people to be loved and attended to, rather than hated or neglected, is again a fact, not a matter of opinion.
>
> *(Warnock 1967: 60)*

For this is irremediably part of our nature, not removable by science fiction. As G. K. Chesterton put it:

> You can imagine any mad botany or geology you please. Think of forests of adamant with leaves of brilliants. Think the moon is a blue moon, a single elephantine sapphire. But don't fancy that all this frantic astronomy would make the smallest difference to the reason and justice of conduct. On plains of opal, under cliffs cut out of pearl, you would still find a notice board, "Thou shalt not steal".
>
> *(Chesterton 1940, quoted in Conway Morris 2003: 313)*

Value, then, is not an extra feature pasted onto the facts by human observers. It is a real emergent property of situations in the world. Each kind of organism acts according to its own values, its own inner design, the characteristic pattern of needs and capacities that determines its direction.

No outside watchmaker, blind or otherwise, is needed to impose these patterns. Natural selection cannot be their main source because – although no doubt it does affect their details – it can only be peripheral. Equally complex patterns are found, after all, throughout nature in inanimate things that do not compete in reproduction at all. Crystals, galaxies, cyclones, rivers and volcanoes all form regularly according to their own established laws without needing to outdo their neighbours. And they all fit together well enough to produce the remarkable degree of order in the world that, so surprisingly, makes science possible and gives rise to the idea of a unifying purpose.

THE MYSTERY OF ORDER

This widespread harmony was what puzzled Darwin when he was wondering about the need for God. What struck him was:

> the extreme difficulty *or rather impossibility* of conceiving this immense and wonderful universe, including man, with his capacity of looking far backward and far into futurity, as the result of blind chance or necessity. When thus reflecting, I feel compelled to look to a First Cause having an intelligent mind in some degree analogous to that of man; and I deserve to be called a Theist.
>
> *(Darwin & Huxley 1974: 54, emphasis added)*

He added, of course, that perhaps we should not trust our human intellects when they draw "such grand conclusions". But then Dawkins's claim to know that there is no such cause is just as grand – just as overconfident – a conclusion as any positive claim that there is one. Extreme negative proposals need just as much support as positive ones. And the alternative notion that DNA somehow stands in for that cause is more overconfident still.

In truth, however, this difficulty about grandeur only affects the *transcendence* of the cause, its metaphysical standing. It does not cast doubt on the order itself or on its immanence – the way it works in the phenomena – which is our present concern. There is nothing unduly grand or fishy about noting that the world is remarkably full of order. Science takes this pervasive order for granted, indeed it relies on it. If we then ask what produces it, and go on to dismiss the suggestion of an outside engineer, it is natural to suppose that order must come from the creativity of matter itself: matter, the silent partner, the piece that is ignored in so many supposedly materialist games of chess.

It turns out, in fact, that Matter is not the inert, passive, standard, characterless stuff of tradition, the mass of standard, lifeless pebbles that seventeenth-century theorists envisaged when they wanted to provide a suitable opposite for spirit and to exile earthly stuff entirely from the business of creation. Instead, matter is something much more active and mysterious; something of which perhaps we actually know very little; something that must have had in it, from the start, the capacity and the tendency to generate all the complexities that have since arisen, and even to rebuild them again after repeated extinctions.

As Nagel has pointed out, "The possibility of the development of conscious organisms must have been built into the world from the beginning. It cannot be an accident" (1994:

68). And Davies, after surveying most thoughtfully the range of views that are possible here, concludes:

> Even though I do not believe Homo sapiens to be more than an accidental by-product of haphazard natural processes... I do believe that life and mind are etched deeply into the fabric of the cosmos, perhaps through a shadowy, half-glimpsed life principle.
>
> *(2006: 302–3)*

Darwin's reasoning does not, of course, call on us to go back to a literal reading of the book of Genesis in order to explain all this self-organizing matter. What it does require is that we recognize intelligence – design – of some kind as a basic constituent of the universe, whatever we may then decide to think about the idea of a designer. What it excludes is the picture of a mindless, meaningless, disconnected system, or rather absence of system.

This non-system, of course, is a picture that many other people besides Dawkins now think of as a safe, sceptical fall-back position, a handy armchair left for them by the Enlightenment. In truth that picture makes no sense, least of all for an age so devoted to science. Human design and purpose are not something extraneous on earth. They are part of this universal order, akin to the rest. Our intelligence is simply one form among many by which wider shaping and ordering capacities – forces that animate and organize the whole cosmos – work in the world.

When we consider something small like a snow crystal we may find it quite natural to see the power of self-organization in this way. We then readily suppose that forces within the stuff it is made of have produced its special shape and quality. But when we come to larger and more complex items such as ourselves, our current way of thinking makes this kind of explanation seem strange and alarming. We are so used to thinking of matter reductively, as something lifeless and alien, that we cannot easily acknowledge it as creative. We then ask anxiously: are these forces supposed to be physical or spiritual?

But is this a sensible question? As Spinoza pointed out, things can be both. Mind and matter are not separate substances; they are complementary aspects of a most complex whole. The gulf that dualists have strenuously dug between these two sides of life has had its uses, but the division is crude and often quite misleading.

Living things are not composites put together out of separate software and hardware. They are complex creatures whose faculties all grow out of their nature as a whole. Such beings need to be thought about in a dozen different ways – not just in two – as we become able to understand their various kinds of complexity better. Trying to explain their evolution reductively in terms of a mere ambition to increase numbers is just a displacement activity. Goodwin, after discussing the many forms of self-organization that have now been found both in living and non-living phenomena, comments:

> A new dimension to fields is emerging from the study of chemical systems such as the Beloussov-Zhabotinsky reaction and the similarity of its spatial patterns to those of living systems. I refer to the emphasis on self-organization, the capacity of these fields to generate patterns spontaneously without any specific instructions telling them what to do, as in a genetic program. These systems produce something out of nothing. Now, we can see precisely what is meant by "nothing" in this context. There is no plan, no blueprint, no instructions about the pattern that emerges. What exists in the field is a set of relationships among the components of the system such that the dynamically stable state into which it goes naturally... has spatial and temporal pattern. Fields of the type we have been considering are now called "excitable media".
>
> (1994: 49)

8

THE BEASTS THAT PERISH

MACHINES ON LEGS

We need here to consider another bad consequence of our traditional dualism – a quite misleading conception of the nature
of non-human animals. This confusion still haunts us, though
it is now under attack. Descartes notoriously ruled that animals
could not be conscious because they were simply automata.
Like his contemporaries he was fascinated by the ingenious
clockwork models that were beginning to be produced in his
day. And, since many of them were actually images of animals,
he readily supposed that real animals could be worked in the
same way. This idea fitted well with the physicists' current view
that all motion was produced by impact, something that cogs
and sprockets could easily produce. It made mechanism seem
a plausible explanation for movement throughout the realm of
nature.

DOI: 10.4324/9781003411710-9

Its drawback was, of course, that it didn't fit the actual behaviour of animals at all. For a clockwork duck to perform the exact movements that have been programmed into it is not at all the same thing as for a real duck to respond flexibly to the unexpected things that happen around her all the time, including, of course, the social signals of her ducklings. Descartes and his contemporaries entirely ignored this business of social signals, even though in practice their whole lives depended on the social signals they constantly exchanged with their horses, and indeed those they exchanged with other humans. It should have struck them that when a sheepdog responds to his master's command, taking the sheep through complicated manoeuvres far off from the signaller, it is hard to see how anybody could explain the process in terms of a clockwork mechanism.

The trouble was that the dualist background only allowed for two alternatives. Animals must either have souls, which would have awkward consequences such as sending them to heaven and entitling them to considerate treatment, or they must simply be material machines. These machines could conveniently be provided in some form like clockwork. No doubt the solution chosen to this dilemma was somewhat influenced by our culture's bias towards meat-eating, and also towards performing scientific experiments. The suggestion (made by a disciple of Descartes) that the screams coming from experimental subjects were merely the insignificant creaking of their rusty mechanism does not sound entirely disinterested. But the materialist view that animals were not conscious still seemed to scientifically minded people for a long time an objective and convincing story.

Voltaire, however, promptly attacked it:

> Barbarians seize this dog, which in friendship surpasses man so prodigiously; they nail it on a table, and they dissect it alive

in order to show the mesemteric veins. You discover in it all the same organs of feeling that are in yourself. Answer me, machinist, *has nature arranged all the means of feeling in this animal, so that it may not feel?* Has it nerves in order to be impassible? Do not suppose this impertinent contradiction in nature.

(Regan & Singer 1976: 67, quoting Voltaire,
Philosophical Dictionary, *"Animals", emphasis added)*

Plenty of people agreed with him and more do today, but the researchers' impression that science demanded belief in the unconsciousness of animals persisted and became increasingly fixed in the tradition.

From a real scientific point of view, however, this belief is surely a mysterious one. What, if anything, is the basis for assuming that Homo sapiens is unique in this respect? The argument about the nerves is surely conclusive. As time went on and evolutionary explanations began to be more widely accepted, the suggestion of an unbridgeable gap in perception between us and all the other animals looked more and more mysterious. Yet animal behaviour has continued for a long time to be studied in these reductive, physicalist terms, as far as possible without any reference to the animals' possible consciousness or their views on what it all meant. The aim has always been to design and report these experiments in a way that would have been appropriate if the subjects had indeed been clockwork automata. Animals, it seemed, did not howl or moan, they "vociferated". They did not "respond" they "reacted". And they never behaved in any way that was not required by the purpose of the experiment.

How persistent this approach has been can be seen from an impressive proclamation called the "Cambridge Declaration on Consciousness", presented as recently as 2012 by a number

of authoritative scientists at (pleasingly enough) the Francis
Crick Memorial Conference on Consciousness in Human and
Non-Human Animals. It testified that they do now think that actually animals may well be conscious. But how do you set about
proving something as obvious as that, something that every
baby knows and which adult experience has never thrown any
doubt on? The compilers face this problem with heroic determination and a load of neurological statistics. At length they
conclude that:

> While comparative research on this topic is naturally ham-
> pered by the inability of non-human animals, and often hu-
> mans, to clearly and readily communicate about their internal
> states, the following observations can be stated unequivocally.
>
> The weight of evidence indicates that humans are not unique
> in possessing the neurological substrates that generate con-
> sciousness. Non-human animals, including all mammals and
> birds, and many other creatures, including octopuses, also
> possess these neurological substrates.
>
> *(Low et al. 2012: 2)*

So they can be conscious (even the octopuses) and when they
act in an intelligent manner, it is reasonable to conclude that
they are.

How can it possibly be necessary to say this today? The admis-
sion certainly comes better late than never, but why has it taken
scientists three hundred years to get rid of an error that a little attention to their own domestic animals could quickly have cured?
As we are beginning to realize, the explanation of this slowness
does not lie in any scientific counter-evidence but in a background myth, a set of assumptions that is essentially religious.

That myth shows humans as exalted above the rest of creation,
not now by the will of God but because their intellectual faculties

allow them to perceive a supersensible semi-divine world – essentially the world of numbers – which forms the explanation of everything. We saw in Chapter 3 where this idea came from and in Chapter 12 we shall encounter some more of its consequences. It teaches us that human uniqueness is not just a matter of being rather different from other species, as elephants or giraffes are. Nor is it only a difference in the mental faculties. It is a metaphysical privilege that sets us altogether apart. That is why doing justice to it has gone on requiring radical dualism just as much as the book of Genesis used to. To prove our distinctness we still need our peculiar ontological status, even though we have lost the worldview that used to support it.

WHAT ABOUT EVOLUTION?

The trouble is, of course, that this sense of separateness is quite incompatible with an evolutionary approach, with a real conviction that all earthly development is gradual and continuous. But it still shouts down that conviction in the souls of the scientistic. This is why accounts of animal behaviour were long required to show it as completely unlike human behaviour and as like as possible to the behaviour of gases. To ensure this, two particularly misleading words have been constantly employed in describing this behaviour: *anecdotal* and *anthropomorphic*.

"Anecdotal" is used to discredit any account of particular concrete events, no matter how well attested it may be. This rule is just an exaggeration of the quite proper requirement that we should support particular accounts by suitable evidence, but, as such single occurrences can at times be really relevant, it is sometimes a serious nuisance. "Anthropomorphic', on the other hand, is a really bad word, one that has long ago escaped from its proper usage into suggesting errors. It originally referred to ideas of God that credited him with having a human shape. When it was transferred to talk about animals, it made sense at first in a particular kind of situation: one where the animals were actually being credited with behaviour that could only be human, as in "a parliament of rooks". But it very quickly came to be used whenever an animal was described in words that would be appropriate for describing a human at all, especially emotion words.

Thus phrases such as "the cat was upset – surprised – terrified or affectionate" had to be translated into strictly behavioural terms, however probable, and indeed however important, it might be that the cat actually did have those feelings. The idea was that, even if the feelings existed, which was still thought to be unlikely, we could not possibly identify them. Claiming to detect them would therefore be anthropomorphism.

This usage simply neglects the fact that *we too are animals* – social animals endowed with good powers of expression – so that both our feelings and the ways in which we express them come directly from our nature and are designed to fit with those of our relatives. All kinds of animals need to be able to read the mood of others around them, not only because those others may pose a threat, or may be food, but also because they may be acquaintances with whom we shall want to socialize, even when they are not of our own species. Racehorses, for instance, often become friendly with a cat or a goat who shares their lodging and they may pine if it is taken away.

The extent to which social signals revealing these moods can be understood across species is indeed somewhat surprising. It shows how deeply we all depend on each other. Warning cries, for instance, are understood everywhere, even across the very deep canyon of evolutionary time that divides mammals from birds. The rich development of these signalling powers on both sides is one of those fascinating convergences that show the shared directions that underlie all of evolution.

All this has, however, been thoroughly neglected until very lately. Darwin, who fully understood its importance, wrote an excellent book about it that he called *The Expression of the Emotions in Man and Animals* (1872). In that book he very properly combined and compared human examples directly with those from other species. For this he used the everyday human language to describe all cases equally, and that language proved perfectly adequate to its task: not surprisingly, since it has been honed for centuries in all kinds of situations, including ones for interspecies communication. (People have always known whether their horses were frightened or angry.) He often pointed out differences between the responses of different species, but he also noted the many close parallels. He drew many of his examples from domestic animals because these were the ones that could be most fully studied in detail. These examples were often "anecdotal" – that is, not repeated – and were used because they were needed to fill in significant details that cast light on a general tendency.

The result of this common-sense approach was that his official followers dismissed the book as the embarrassing lapse of an ageing investigator – an amateur clearly tainted by folk psychology – and said as little as possible about it during his centenary celebrations. They thought it unscientific. How wrong this was is surely now clear. That stress on our natural powers of communication was just what was needed in order to shake up the absurd isolation in which the human race was still supposed to be existing. It cuts through some of the partitions that have been erected to divide us from the rest of nature. It shows that, peculiar and sublime though we may be in some ways, we can still feel at home on the earth alongside its other inhabitants, instead of having no company except numbers.

Plenty of people can appreciate that approach. And it ought at once to have been followed up after Darwin's book came out. But it wasn't, and it was some time before his example was really followed. At the beginning of the twentieth century the behaviourists, then ruling psychology, brushed it aside and constantly supported their doctrines by research on animals that was conducted entirely on artificial mechanistic principles. They silenced any other suggestions.

REALISM ABOUT ANIMALS

The scientist who eventually broke this monopoly and produced a more realistic approach was Konrad Lorenz, an Austrian ethologist who understood animals deeply and did not care in the least what his colleagues thought of him. Writing in the 1930s, he described the life of geese, jackdaws and other creatures clearly and directly, using everyday psychological language as Darwin had done, and using it – just as Darwin did – so intelligently that anybody could see it was appropriate to the animals. His friend Niko Tinbergen did the same good service for gulls and other birds. Their example launched a whole new tradition of vigorous animal studies in which people like Jane Goodall responded directly to the thoughts and wishes of the animals while still supplying plenty of scientific detail.

This was a drastic change. When Goodall first started to write about chimpanzee behaviour, her supervisor told her at once to stop referring to her animals by names. Scientific procedure required her to use only numbers. She replied that names made it much easier to remember the events – something that had indeed already been established by other psychologists – and eventually he reluctantly allowed her to go on doing so. Now, of course, investigators do it all the time.

This episode shows the extraordinary power of dualist habits. In theory, dualism was already becoming discredited at this time; the movement was already towards materialism. But the dualist myth was still strong, presenting its imaginative picture of a divided world, a world in which animals loomed on the non-human side of a stark division as menacing extras, needing to be controlled. To suit this picture, many people still thought it was a basic scientific truth that animals were, in a peculiar sense, things: things in a way that people were not.

The behaviourists, when they were feeling strong, dealt with this awkward situation drastically by saying that, of course, humans were only things too. As Skinner put it, "We should not be anthropomorphic about man". Most of the time, however, they had to allow some space to the mental story in studying people. Why didn't they do so about other species? The reason for this was extremely simple; they were too ignorant about them to see the point at all.

Lorenz's contribution was crucial here. By filling in some of the real details about animals he cleared away the symbolic fantasies that had gathered around them, fantasies expressed by the associations attached to words such as rat, snake, wolf, cow, bitch, ape, raven, crocodile, shark and so forth. He showed that these fancies bore no relation to the actual behaviour of the creatures. Wolves, for instance, display all the domestic virtues and do not go ravening out of savagery but simply for survival. The beasts were being used as figures onto which all sorts of fears and fantasies could be projected.

By describing their actual lives more fully, Lorenz showed not just that they were less dangerous than we thought but that they were not the frighteningly alien beings that people imagined. They were normal fellow inhabitants of the earth. They are, he said, much more like us emotionally than we have supposed, although they are often less like us intellectually. This new understanding made it possible for people to share their world with animals imaginatively rather than trying to get rid of them. It showed nature itself as a system that we could well be part of, rather than as an alien force against which we had to fight. (The need to wage a "war against nature" had been a favourite theme of thinkers in the early twentieth century, notably Freud and William James.)

This change was crucial, not just because it improved our relations with the animals but because it made us more aware of our own vulnerability, of the pace at which we were damaging our planet. Throughout the nineteenth century and much of the twentieth, most influential people in the West simply did not consider this at all. The environmental costs of the Industrial Revolution scarcely crossed their minds. When their attention was drawn to particular kinds of damage, their reassuring answer was always that science and technology would be able to find cures for any harm they might happen to do. They thought that civilization was self-perpetuating. The dualist world picture that showed us as observers and engineers, organizing from a distance a scene over which we had total authority, left no room for the thought that we ourselves could be in real danger.

If we had not been ruled by that picture – if we had had a more realistic vision of our relation to the earth – we would surely have understood much more quickly the harm that we were doing. Here again it is striking to notice how myths – imaginative visions – can stop people from seeing plainly visible facts. And the interesting point about this particular case is that it was the myth – not the facts – that was deemed to be scientific. For a long time, talk about planetary damage was dismissed as fanciful – sentimental, frilly, feminine – "new age", even though it often came from well-qualified scientists.

The trouble is that what people were used to thinking of as scientific was the mechanistic vision in which nothing could really go wrong. That vision is still powerful today, notably in the USA where it does most damage, but also in countries like the UK where, although we may believe the news about the danger, droughts and floods have not yet brought that message home.

What all this means is that our belief in our detachment from the other animals, and from the earth that has produced them, is surely one more example of what may well be called scientistic superstition: an opinion maintained by convention contrary to well-known evidence in order to suit an imaginative habit. As far as animals are concerned, this notion differs from some others in that, at least in certain situations, it does seem to be seriously believed. Meat-eating and uncontrolled animal experimentation are indeed activities consistent with the idea that animals are unconscious, although they may well not be consistent with people's attitudes towards their cats and horses. Similarly, the belief that earth cannot be hurt by our abuse is consistent with our policy of doing hardly anything to protect it, although not, of course, with the news about it that we are getting every day. But there are other parts of these strange pseudoscientific conventions that quite plainly are not seriously believed since they do not produce appropriate behaviour. The most striking of these is the denial of free will.

9

FREE WILL, NOT JUST FREE WON'T

FREE FROM WHAT?

We have seen that one important consequence of ignoring subjectivity is its effect on the topic of free will, which, as Crick rightly said, is a crucial aspect of our self-image. Materialists flatly deny that there is any such thing as free will, dismissing it as a necessary illusion with a certainty that has made this denial a cliché of pseudoscientific talk. Thus, as we have seen, Blakemore rules confidently that "it makes no sense (in scientific terms) to distinguish sharply between acts that result from conscious attention and those that result from our reflexes or damage to the brain".

The difference between these two kinds of acts is, however, glaring and central to all human social life. The distinction

DOI: 10.4324/9781003411710-10

between deliberate choices and those that are forced upon people matters crucially to all of us; it constantly shapes and reshapes our social relations. So this dismissal of it is surely one more example of the sort of unrealistic convention that we have been considering.

People give various reasons for dismissing free will as unscientific. Mostly, however, these flow from a very common but superstitious and highly anthropomorphic view of *causality as compulsion*, a melodramatic picture of causes as manipulators forcing helpless objects to produce their effects. Thus the brain cells are conceived as pushing levers that, from outside, compel the mind to write mc^2, rather than the mind's working the problem out for itself.

This idea of causation by a sequence of separate events is, however, actually quite foreign to science. Even when cause and effect are apparently separate, as when lightning causes a bush fire, there is no drama of compulsion because there is no resistance. The idea of lightning as forcing the wood to burn might well have a place in poetry, but from a scientific angle it is irrelevant. The whole process is simply part of a regular sequence, much like the earth's rotation or the growth of a plant, in which nobody detects compulsion. And the same is true of the parts played by thought and brain function in mental activity.

What, however, does the idea of free will actually involve? It is not just a name for a general exemption from causality. Essentially it concerns *effort*, which is a perfectly real causal factor. It does not call on us to claim that outside causes of action don't exist or that they have no effect on thought. It simply means that they should be treated as the partial factors that they are, not as all-powerful tsunamis that must overwhelm mental strivings and intentions. It means that our efforts can in principle be effective; that thoughts have their real place among other kinds of causes in the world.

Thus, if someone whose ageing brain finds it hard to remember numbers tries hard to recall a particular number and succeeds, the states of that brain are indeed an important part of the background conditions. But so are the efforts made, and these can determine the result one way or another. Again, if a persistent person (perhaps Einstein again?) is trying to solve a problem, the efforts he makes, and the peculiar direction his recent thinking gives to those efforts, determine results that could not possibly have occurred on their own without this attention.

Something that clashes with current orthodoxy must be said plainly here. *Minds can affect brains as well as brains affecting minds.* Thoughts can directly alter the state of the brain cells. Thus, when Einstein makes his calculation, his decision to use a certain method will surely bring about new patterns of cell arrangement, which would not have been there if he had decided otherwise. This link was illustrated by the case of the London taxi-drivers whose hippocampi turned out to have become enlarged as a result of memorizing the map of the city. In fact, of course, the new thought and the cerebral rearrangement are not separate events. They are aspects of a single activity that we perceive in two separate ways, just as we do in the case of sight and touch or of lightning and thunder.

In order to understand such decisions, we need to grasp that our choices are not only about *whether* to do something already set before us. Much more often they are about *what to do.* We have to attend to our whole situation and to keep thinking about the many ways in which we might deal with it. Our decisions about this, even if they often take us in very ordinary directions, form the shape of our lives.

If somebody could become convinced that their free will really was an illusion, that their thoughts were quite ineffective – which, luckily, most people can't – they would then become a helpless full-time fatalist. They would probably try to stop thinking and would not be able to act. But this dismal destiny would not have been brought about by fate, nor indeed by their neurons. It would result from their own bad choices, formed by their own thinking.

THERE ARE ALWAYS THOUGHTS

This wide range of mental possibilities is often obscured by arguments drawn from highly artificial cases that have been deliberately simplified so as to leave only minimal choice open. Thus, in the experiments described by Benjamin Libet, which are widely taken to disprove free will, the subject is simply asked to raise his hand at a moment of his own choice. When he has done this, investigations apparently show that brain motions preparatory to this move occurred very slightly before he was aware of choosing to act. From this Libet concluded that the brain was the responsible party that took the initiative and that it merely imposed this decision on the conscious mind.

It has always struck me as extraordinary that, in these experiments, nobody seems to have taken the trouble to ask the subjects what they had been thinking about before they made their movements. Had they done so, the subjects would surely have had answers to give. They might have said something like, "Well, I was thinking, that's probably about five minutes, is that enough?", or "My elbow was itching', or "I'd finished counting up to 100", or simply, "I was getting bored".

It doesn't matter how slight the explanation is. The point is that the act emerged, as all conscious acts do, from a substantial context of motivation that formed a background preparatory to action. This process of formation has various stages, both mental and cerebral, in which the explicit consciousness of the decision and the movement itself are only elements. They are not separate events and certainly not reflex actions. The order in which these elements of preparation occur (or rather in which they reach the recording instruments) seems, therefore, a relatively trivial matter, certainly too trivial to support the conclusion that the brain movement was the sole cause of the mental decision.

Thus, even in this painfully thin case, preparatory thoughts play a crucial part in producing the action. Just as we saw in the more complex examples that I have deliberately used so far – examples where the decisions to be made plainly involve mental work such as calculation – so, even in simpler, everyday cases, the mental stream leading to action is always needed. It moves alongside the cerebral one and is constantly in touch with it; they form part of a single activity. But neither can be reduced to the other. They are parts of a single process. It is interesting that Libet himself seems to have had some suspicion of this since he is recorded to have said that although there is no free will, *"perhaps there is free won't"*. This rather oracular remark suggests a sense of the need to gesture towards everyday experience. But, of course, it is not sufficient to clear up the matter.

NOT A STRING OF BEADS

What, then, is causality? Attempts like Libet's to line up these two events as physical cause and mental effect mostly grow from a distorted conception of causality itself as a single linear sequence, a string of beads in which each event simply sets off the one that follows it, as if by impact. Indeed the word "cause" itself is sometimes taken to mean merely a unit in this kind of linear sequence. That word, however, like *aitia*, the word that corresponds to it in Greek, originally had the wider meaning of explanation, and it still often does so. Explanations come in many forms, varying with the kind of question that needs to be asked at the time. Thus my local buses rightly tell me "not to speak to the driver without good cause". Relevant explanation often involves giving reasons.

Aristotle originally made this clear in a passage that is now, most misleadingly, called "Aristotle's doctrine of the four causes", but which is actually a discussion of four kinds of explanation: four "*becauses*"; four kinds of question that may be asked about a thing.

For instance (keeping to the familiar case of the table) we may ask what it is made of and the answer is wood, plastic or whatever. This is its matter and can be called the "material cause". Then we ask about its shape and other details and the answer gives us its "formal cause". Third comes the "efficient cause", which is the event that set it off. This, of course, is what the word *cause* most often means today and the question seems much more appropriate when we are asking about the source of an *event* (such as a lightning strike) than when we ask about a table. We can, however, give the table an efficient cause by describing its construction. Fourth comes the case in which the mistranslation has been a real disaster, the "final cause". This phrase simply means "explanation by purpose", that is, by detecting the end or aim (*telos*) of the thing. The question that is being asked here is probably the first and simplest one that would occur to someone who knew nothing about the object in question, namely "What's it for?" (after all, not all cultures use tables).

This is a question that constantly arises about all sorts of man-made objects, and it was one of Aristotle's best discoveries that it is also a useful question to ask about natural objects. In observing and dissecting many sorts of animals, he constantly found that their various parts seemed to do some sort of work (*ergon*), that they were not just chance growths but organs (*organa*, tools) playing a necessary part in their life. By tracing these functions he was able to get a better understanding of the creatures' lives. And, since Greek thought did not use the idea of a divine creator, he was never tempted to suggest that these functions expressed the purposes of an outside planner.

Thus Aristotelian teleology is not, as people often suppose, just one more version of the biblical creation story. Instead it starts from the basic, primitive question about each particular, "What's this for?" and proceeds by looking for whatever outcomes can, in the particular context, be intelligibly seen as advantages. By doing this systematically it begins to understand these various functions as parts of larger wholes, systems within which the relation between the various parts continually makes better sense of them. That's what Darwin was doing when he devised his evolutionary system based on natural selection. The trouble was that he stopped there. He didn't go on half long enough, and his paralysis has been transmitted in spades to his followers.

It is not surprising that people have not been willing to trace out the details of all these various sorts of "causality", which are really kinds of explanation. Natural sequences do, of course, often seem to present the simple linear causal pattern when we look at them from a distance. Lightning does set off wildfires, cancer sets off death. But a nearer approach always calls for a less simple analysis, showing the wider context and the longer process within which these things happen. Much of causality proceeds by larger, more continuous and intelligible progressions, as in the movements of planets or the growth of plants. And, where human action is involved, no explanation that does not involve motives answers the appropriate questions at all.

I should perhaps say a word here about a defence that is sometimes mounted for exclusively physical explanation: the idea that reasonings themselves are not independent because they in turn arise from physical causes. This, of course, calls first for a simple *tu quoque* reply; those physical causes may in their turn have had mental causes, and so on forever. But, more seriously, the point is that, as I have argued in all these cases, thoughts need to spring from further thoughts that are *relevant*. If you want the explanation of a particular piece of reasoning, the only place to look for it is in other relevant reasonings. Blaming the neurons for it instead will get you nowhere.

10

HOW DIVIDED SELVES LIVE

ONE THING NOT TWO: WITHIN AND WITHOUT

We have seen that the claim to eliminate free will has many things wrong with it. But one striking thing it has in common with attempts to eliminate the self is, as I have been suggesting, that neither of them seems to be at all seriously meant. Rejecting free will normally makes no change in the rejecters' lives. They don't believe the denial that they profess. If, for instance, they lose an important document, they do not refuse to think where they left it, on the grounds that their mental efforts can never affect the world. Nor do they complain when it is assumed that the winners of Nobel prizes ought to work to deserve them, or that plagiarists ought not to steal other people's results.

Materialists, like everybody else, take it for granted that conscious decisions and conscious efforts ceaselessly determine

DOI: 10.4324/9781003411710-11

our actions. Responsibility cannot possibly be an illusion. It is one of the hinges on which our world turns. It is not (as some people think) an intrusion produced by religion; it is just one of the roots out of which religion – along with many other things – can develop.

This common-sense recognition of agency supports neither materialism nor dualism. What it tells us is that the entity who actually decides things is neither the brain nor an alien spirit within us. It has to be the whole person: the inclusive being of whom that brain is a part. This being uses the brain to make decisions just as he or she uses other parts, such as arms and legs to move with.

Our puzzles about the relation of mind and body are real enough. But they are not metaphysical puzzles about the relation between two competing entities litigating for possession of the privileged title "reality". They are practical puzzles about how to relate two parts or aspects of ourselves: the inside and the outside of the teapot; the living subject who actually has the experiences and the archivist or librarian who keeps trying to describe them in terms that other people can understand.

In fact, *a human being is one thing, not two*. But this one thing is very complex and, for a number of reasons, people have split it up in various ways, producing different maps of it, of which our traditional pattern of matter and spirit is just one. When these maps are clearly laid out they can look quite factual – quite like an objective analysis of a rock into its various ingredients. But they are really much more dependent on the observer's assumptions, much more like the highly partial accounts that we constantly give of human motives. They describe what can be seen from a particular point of view. As Iain McGilchrist says:

> Descartes was right; the one undeniable fact is our consciousness. He was wrong, however, most would now agree, to think

of mind and body as two separate substances (two "whats"). This was, I believe, a typical product of a certain way of thinking which I suggest is characteristic of the brain's left hemisphere, a concern with the "whatness" of things. Where it was so obviously a matter of two "hownesses" in the same thing, two different modes of being (as the right hemisphere would see it), he could formulate this only as two whatnesses, two different things.... *Mind has the characteristics of a process more than of a thing; a becoming, a way of being rather than an entity.*

(2009: 20, emphasis added)

The point about the left hemisphere will be discussed more fully in Chapter 11. It is that, roughly speaking the left half of the brain is the detailed, obsessive part; the right half is the one that can look at things as a whole. The two always need to cooperate and this need is most urgent when a point of view that is widely accepted is becoming registered as a wider, more official world picture: a metaphysic, an organized map of life as a whole, a general story that can be taken as a truth.

Thus, what made Descartes and his colleagues suggest our current form of dualism in the seventeenth century was essentially their wish to accommodate the rising practice of science in their world without disturbing the religious background, which in general they accepted. And, since they were rationalists – deeply convinced of the power of reasoning, deeply partial to left-hemisphere thinking – they expressed their dualistic view in confident terms as a universal metaphysical truth. They concentrated on making it tidy rather than comprehensive.

Since that time so many elements of this landscape have shifted that it does not fit our life neatly as it once did, which is why it is no longer officially accepted. There are, however, various reasons for dividing the self that have survived this change. We still find that we perceive this very complex being, the self, in two distinct ways. There is an everyday split between our inner and outer viewpoint: between what we directly feel and what we believe to be true of the world. Roughly speaking, mind and body are names that correspond with what we perceive in these two ways.

But the meaning we attach to these names is still shaped by our metaphysical worldview. Descartes, one of the first philosophers to take notice of this distinctive inner sense of ourselves, identified it promptly with the soul, the religiously recognized form of spirit. This had startling consequences. It meant that the soul was immortal and that its true home was in heaven, not on earth. Moreover, it was radically separate from the body: separate, therefore, from the whole earth around it. Descartes emphasized this separateness, insisting that matter was inert, neutral stuff understandable only from outside through the laws of physics, which was, of course, the field in which the first wave of modern scientific thinking was achieving its most striking successes.

This metaphysical creed could not, however, get rid of the close connection between mind and body. That connection puzzled Descartes very much. At one point he wrote that it was not like the relation between a boat and the person who sails it, but most of what he wrote about it suggests that it was, indeed, exactly like that. At the end of the voyage the sailor will pack up and go home, leaving the boat to a quite separate fate.

The gap between our inner and outer views of the world is indeed a real one. These two ways of confronting it are as distinct as the two main ways by which we perceive the physical things around us: sight and touch. Here, too, our two sources of knowledge usually agree so well that we can treat their messages as continuous. But their differences are sometimes important and we should not assume that one of them is always right. This is rather like our perception of lightning and thunder, where we both see and hear a single electric discharge in distinct ways through our two separate senses. Here, too, it would obviously be misleading to assume that only one sense reveals the truth and must always prevail.

When two kinds of perception seem to clash like this – as they do, for instance, over optical illusions – we have to find some way of deciding which should prevail. And that is why we frame our worldviews, sketch maps that are necessarily imaginative compromises between inner and outer perception. Dualism itself is, of course, one such map, but it is one that cannot really be taken as final. Not only is the relation between its two parts obscure, but there is clearly something odd about its neglect of the obvious middle term: Life. As Margulis noted, earlier thinking had found a place for life quite easily:

> Organic beings and environment... interweave. Soil, for instance, is not unalive. It is a mixture of broken rock, pollen, fungal filaments, ciliate cysts, bacterial spores, nematodes and other microscopic animals and their parts. "Nature" Aristotle observed, "proceeds little by little from things lifeless to animal life in such a way that it is impossible to determine the exact line of demarcation." *Independence is a political, not a scientific term.*
>
> *(1995: 26, quoting Aristotle,*
> The History of Animals, *viii, 1, emphasis added)*

I thought of this lately when I heard a would-be space-colonizer insisting that we must quickly begin to study Martian soil so as to provide for our future agriculture when we go there. That, I thought, is going to be rather easy; there isn't any soil. Since that time, too, I have noticed more than one expert advising these colonists that they must "use local resources" or "live off the land".

WHAT IS IT TO BE SCIENTIFIC?

People today find it hard to see this sort of point. They don't grasp our total dependence on and continuity with the earth around us, even when that dependence is very obvious, just as they find it hard to believe in climate change even when they are living in it. The reason in both cases is that the assumptions about what is "scientific" that they have grown up with leave no room for such possibilities.

This is largely because the pioneers of modern science, such as Descartes, Galileo and the men of the Royal Society, abandoned the earlier Aristotelian sensitivity to the earth's continuity with its inhabitants, replacing it by a sharp, dramatic division between matter and spirit, which consigned the earth as a whole to the realm of inert matter. They deliberately intensified the contrast between humans – whom they ranked with spirit – and the rest of creation, which was merely matter for humans to work on. They were particularly keen to get rid of the whole imagery of natural magic, a force that many serious scholars in their day regarded as crucial in the creation and preservation of life.

For instance Copernicus, when he cited ancient authorities to support his thesis in the introduction to his book, readily listed among others the Egyptian sage Hermes Trismegistus, who, as Wertheim explains, was:

> not a mathematician or an astronomer but a magician; in fact, he was considered the source of Western magic...
>
> During the fifteenth and sixteenth centuries it [magic] was considered a legitimate science of nature. To Copernicus and his contemporaries, magic was a real power based on legitimate and subtle understanding of the hidden forces of nature.
>
> While it was widely acknowledged that mathematics was useful for describing the celestial realm... Magic, on the other

hand seemed to offer genuine insight into a broad spectrum of nature....

The difference between "science" and "magic" was not always so clear as it seems to us today... Magic's acquisition of a new legitimacy during the Renaissance made it, for a time, the leading competitor to Aristotelian science... The magi went out into society and put their craft to use. In particular they were employed at Renaissance courts.

(1997: 82–3)

In fact, magic was for a time considered to be the practical art relevant for understanding things on earth, from alchemy to medicine, even if not in the heavens. It operated with an organic philosophy of nature in which the world was seen as a living organism with a material body and an immaterial "world soul", which could be influenced by those who understood it. And since the word for soul is feminine, this soul was taken to be female. If we ask how it works, Marsilio Ficino explains it thus:

All the power of magic consists in love... The work of magic is the attraction of one thing by another in virtue of their natural sympathy. The parts of the world, like the members of one animal... are united among themselves in the community of a single nature. From their communal relationship a common love is born and from this love a common attraction, and this is the true magic... Thus the loadstone attracts iron, amber, straw, brimstone, fire; the Sun draws leaves and flowers towards itself, the moon, the seas.

(Ficino 1956)

This general assumption about the importance of attraction is surely just as rational a place to start from as the contrary one, popular today, that the universal force is competition. Both need, of course, to be checked in particular cases, and the particular phenomena that Ficino mentioned were ones that really could not be explained mechanistically through the mere clashing of particles impacting on one another, which was the only force allowed by the new physics. Galileo, for instance, refused to consider Kepler's suggestion that the tides were produced by attraction to the moon because he regarded attraction itself as a superstitious concept. He insisted instead on an obscure explanation involving impacts.

No attempt, then, was made to bring the two approaches together. Instead, both were hotly defended, not just as scientific doctrines but also as paths to salvation. Ficino took pains to point out that the art of magic was not demonic but only invoked natural forces. Yet, like Pythagoreanism, this creed too had a strong religious element:

> The practice of magic was viewed as a "holy quest', a search for knowledge, not by study and research but by revelation. "The art of magic is the art of worshipping God" wrote Sir Walter Raleigh... Some educated practitioners actually sought out village wise women and learned from them; notably Paracelsus, the famed sixteenth-century alchemist who spent his life championing the common people... But by the end of the century the clerical tide was increasingly turning against occult arts of all varieties. The late sixteenth and early seventeenth centuries was the time of the great European witchhunts.
>
> *(Wertheim 1997: 88–9)*

Thus the rivalry that had been developing between the idea of natural magic and the new physics was finally resolved in the physicists' favour. No doubt this was partly because of the strength of their theories, but it was also because the religious sensibilities of the age had changed. Any talk of love or sympathy that was not involved with the Christian God was now rejected with disgust. Nature had come under grave suspicion as a supposedly rival deity that must be debunked.

HERESY-HUNTING BEGINS

This, then, was primarily a victory of one mythology over another and the victors eagerly celebrated it in the appropriate mythological terms. Robert Boyle complained with disgust that, "Men are taught and wont to attribute stupendous unaccountable effects... to a certain being... which they call nature, for this is represented as... a kind of goddess, whose powers may be little less than boundless" (Boyle 1722: vol. 5, 532). Francis Bacon had already declared war on this person in highly dramatic language, writing that we should not merely "exert a gentle guidance over Nature's course", which, of course, is much what would be recommended today, but should "conquer and subdue her, to shake her to her foundations". Scientists, he added, must turn "with united forces against the Nature of Things, to storm and occupy her castles and strongholds... and subdue Nature with all her children to bind her to your service and make her your slave". This, he claimed, would set off a new epoch, which he rather oddly called a "masculine birth of time" (Farrington 1970). Joseph Glanvill made the point in an interestingly different way, shifting the emphasis from the mythical figure of Nature to the scientists' own inner psychology – to the dangerous clash between Reason and Feeling:

> Where the Will, or Passion, hath the casting vote, the case of Truth is desperate....
>
> *(1970: 118)*

> The Woman in us, still prosecutes a Deceit like that begun in the garden, and our understandings are wedded to an Eve, as fatal as the mother of our miseries. And while things are

> judged according to their suitableness, or disagreement to the
> gusto of the fond Feminine, we shall be as far from the tree of
> knowledge as from that guarded by the Cherubim.
>
> *(Ibid.: 135)*

If we notice that this extraordinarily theatrical stuff was the everyday talk of the founders of modern science, we shall, I think, find it easier to understand why their twentieth-century descendants reacted with such startling violence in the 1960s when James Lovelock first put forward his conception of Gaia. His suggestion that biologists could learn something by viewing the earth, along with its plants and animals, as in certain ways like a whole organism, a cohesive community acting to develop itself harmoniously – that this vision would be more useful than treating every species as a separate and competing individual and that we ourselves were part of this community – was a perfectly sensible scientific proposal. Indeed, it was the natural progression from Darwin's conception of the balance of nature.

Lovelock backed this idea with a number of well-supported scientific proposals that showed the continuity, and the mutual dependence, between the earth and the living things upon it. The best known of these is perhaps the way in which plankton in the ocean sends particles of dimethyl sulphide into the air, particles that act as seeds for water vapour to condense into clouds, thus speeding up the water cycle. There is also the chemical weathering by which rocks interact with the air's carbon dioxide, producing solid carbonate compounds that eventually find their way to the ocean floor, thus contributing to cooling the climate. This weathering can take place on its own, but the presence of living things raises the speed of the process between ten- and a hundredfold. It thus stores away a lot of carbon. There is also the supply of oxygen, little of which existed on the earth's surface in pure form until green plants began to produce it through photosynthesis. This made possible an immense extension of life forms and thereby many changes in the earth itself, such as the generation of soil. And this continued work by green plants is still necessary to allow life to continue (Holmes 2013a).

All these phenomena, and many more like them, show the immense importance of something that dualism had not just overlooked but had deemed to be impossible: the spontaneous activity of earthly matter, working in its most active form, life. Without this array of animating processes our planet would have remained, like Mars and Venus, an inert lump of rock, either roasting hot or freezing cold, and – even if still interesting – totally uninhabitable. Nor, of course, would we have been present to complain about it. This dependence, this continuity of our species with the earth it lives on, is something we badly need to understand so as to get a realistic idea of our own position, notably, of how vulnerable we are to the earth's misfortunes, how far we are from living in the distant security of that pure observer whom our myth envisaged.

Thus Lovelock's suggestion was not at all disreputable scientifically. But when it first appeared biologists rejected it in startlingly strong language. John Maynard Smith called it "an evil religion"; Paul Ehrlich described Lovelock as "radical and dangerous" and Robert May called him "a holy fool" (Bond 2013: 48). After a time this panic calmed down and eventually, indeed, a good deal of this Gaian thinking has been widely accepted among scientists. In fact, universities now standardly run departments of "earth science", a name that is based on this idea. Maynard Smith himself explained this situation to Lovelock by saying, "All the trouble with Gaia is that we've had such agony with vitalism and group-selection and all these other things, and we thought we had it all worked out, and then you came along. You couldn't have chosen a worse moment" (quoted in *ibid.*). In short, the Church Scientific (as T. H. Huxley shrewdly called it) was plagued with heresies and it couldn't be bothered to discriminate between them. Since that time, however, group selection has (as we have seen) been accepted as scientifically respectable and, although vitalism (the belief in an independent life-force) was indeed usually very crude, the reasons that led people to propose it still need our attention today.

So the basic ideas behind Gaian thinking are working their way into general acceptance. But what is still not accepted – what still gives these scientists the shivers – is the *name* "Gaia". The symbolism of that name, which compared the earth to a nourishing divine mother, made perfectly good sense to the general public when it was first proposed, just as it had done to the ancient Greeks who first used it. The implication that *we ourselves are dependants,* small, vulnerable beings who receive this bounty spontaneously as children do and that we need to treat its sources with due respect, made sense at once to many people and is now beginning to be widely understood. But the natural way of expressing it – the obvious metaphor of a family – still stands outside the mythological context that currently goes with the word "scientific', and the feminine imagery still seems dangerously alien. The profession of physics is still seen as a kind of priesthood, from which profane and unfamiliar aspirants must be carefully excluded.

As we shall see in Chapter 12 this sense of a special mission has deep roots in a tradition that goes back to Plato and Pythagoras. The imaginative gender barrier that it produces may well be part of the reason why physicists have for a long time been particularly resistant to accepting women as colleagues. From the seventeenth century, when a few educated women began to want to work on the subject, the scientific community barred their entry to the profession whenever possible, far more firmly than did the communities of most of the other sciences. And even when they did find their way in they tended not to be fully accepted. Thus, even when Marie Curie had received her Nobel Prize, gossip in the profession still suggested for a long time that the work credited to her had really been done by her husband.

There is also surely no doubt that today's still persistent climate change denial is powered from the same source: that it draws on the same scientistic superstitions about human safety and superiority. Although this resistance is not phrased in ideological terms – although it is mostly defended today on the grounds that predictions of climate disaster cannot be proved for certain – these claims to uncertainty are so thin that the resistance is plainly ideological.

NATURICIDE AND DEICIDE

The general point that comes out from all this is that our thinking today is still shaped, far more than we realize, by the zeal with which these seventeenth-century reformers dismissed the whole idea of an active, creative Nature. For both religious and philosophical reasons they declared this a pagan fancy. They held that all real activity came directly from a single source, God, thus ensuring both the world's goodness and – what was even more important – its rational coherence. All other movement came simply from mechanical impact and could be studied by physicists in terms of quantities.

As Descartes put it, "There exist no occult forces in stones or plants. There are no amazing sympathies and antipathies, in fact there exists nothing in the whole of nature which cannot be explained by purely corporeal causes totally devoid of mind and thought" (*Principles of Philosophy*, §187). These are the assumptions that enabled physics to isolate its subject matter by abstraction from all the surrounding conceptual scenery, and, of course, thereby to make astonishing progress in its chosen direction.

This demotion of Nature was, in fact, another of those intellectual earthquakes I mentioned earlier, occasions when familiar beliefs are suddenly discredited and new ones taken for granted. And since this particular earthquake was the one that established what we still call "modern science", we still live with the assumptions which established that science's triumphs as permanent.

It is interesting, however, that one of those assumptions has since dropped out entirely from the scientific scene, almost unmentioned. The omnipotent God who was central to the cosmos of Galileo and Newton is gone, and this is a real change. Galileo's troubles with the Church never disturbed his theism; they were essentially political. And in general, references to God in scientific writings of that time are not (as people now sometimes think) just a matter of form. As well as expressing real devoutness they have a strong controversial punch. They were emphasized to discredit the old dependence on Nature as an outdated superstition. God, in fact, was there to displace nature and provide (it was hoped) a fully intelligible cosmos.

There was, however, always a difficulty in seeing how this arrangement could keep spirit and body cooperating harmoniously forever. Would not one realm simply have to eat up the other in the end? People readily supposed that, as St Paul unfortunately put it, "the flesh warreth against the Spirit and the Spirit against the flesh", and as time went on they took sides with whichever seemed likely to win. It was this sense of competition that later made the simple removal of mind seem like a plausible solution. And it is this same sense of competition that still leads us to dramatize the relations between our inner and outer life, for instance when trying to decide which to concentrate on in cases of mental illness, or even when trying to resolve our inner conflicts.

This is important because these inner conflicts are, of course, a crucial aspect of our lives. They always make it hard to consider the self as, indeed, a single whole. Yet this wholeness – this "integration of the personality" as Jung called it – is essential to all our thinking, including our ordinary personal lives. We do not have the option of really turning into pairs of separate people. Nor, of course, do we have a complete, organized unity, as a simple machine might. But we each have within us an ongoing unifying enterprise, a more-or-less workable inner polity. We are often busy in reconciling its endemic conflicts. And there are various aspects of our lives that do make us feel divided. We should perhaps look here at one more of these oddities: the strange doubleness of our brains.

11

HEMISPHERES AND HOLISM

DIFFERENT KINDS OF ATTENTION

It is really interesting to consider the complexities that are now emerging about the workings of our two cerebral hemispheres. This is one more context in which we may feel divided, and one that we very much need to understand. As we have seen, in this case the relation between our experience and the neuroscientific facts is rather different from that in most others. Over these hemispheres, neurology does not just give us a new, interesting piece of knowledge, it actually casts light on puzzles that are already making trouble in our lives. The detailed facts here light up the meaning of various oppositions that we already recognize as features of our culture and that we often find hard to deal with: oppositions such as the clash between classical and romantic, between feeling and reason, between science and religion, between body and mind, between the arts

DOI: 10.4324/9781003411710-12

and sciences, between amateur and professional, between male and female. This does not, of course, mean that the two brain hemispheres simply represent the two named parties that clash in these debates. What they represent is distinctive attitudes, distinctive ways of viewing and apprehending the world. As McGilchrist says:

> Both hemispheres are involved in almost all mental processes, and certainly in all mental states;... But, *at the level of experience*, the world we know is synthesized from the work of the two cerebral hemispheres, each hemisphere having its own way of understanding the world – its own "take" on it... Though I would resist the idea of a "(left or right) hemisphere personality" overall, there is evidence... that certainly for some kinds of activities, we consistently prefer one hemisphere over the other in ways that may differ between individuals.
>
> *(McGilchrist 2009: 10, original emphasis)*

So how does this work? We are now familiar with pictures of the brain that show how similar its two halves are, and also how there are many slight differences between them. Researchers studying these were at first puzzled by this strange duplication because they found it hard to see that the right hemisphere was doing any work at all. The left half seemed to be much better at solving the kind of intelligence tests that readily occurred to them; so it was taken to be in charge and was at first called the "dominant hemisphere".

Further investigation, however, showed that this is wrong. Patients with injuries to the right side of their brain turned out not to be at all in a balanced and satisfactory condition. Their left brain did indeed often show various detailed skills, especially with words, but it often could not envisage the situation as a whole – indeed, it could not even see that this wider perspective might be needed. The right brain, however little it might talk, was the one that observed this broader background and considered on the whole what ought to be done next.

In fact, a person who was dominated by their left brain was rather in the position of an archaeologist digging in a very deep hole and quite unwilling to stop doing so in order to check on the site as a whole, unable even to listen when someone above them is shouting down that the whole site is in danger of immediate flooding. (As I mentioned earlier, this was probably the sort of behaviour that caused Pliny the Elder to get killed when he was so eagerly investigating the eruption of Vesuvius.)

That difference between the two is not, of course, a difference in capacity. It is a difference in attitude, in the way we attend to our surroundings. McGilchrist comments:

> The kind of attention we pay actually alters the world; we are, literally, partners in creation... Many of the disputes about the nature of the human world can be illuminated by an understanding that there are two fundamentally different "versions" delivered to us by the two hemispheres, both of which can have a ring of authenticity about them, and both of which are hugely valuable, but that they stand in opposition to one another and need to be kept apart – hence the bicameral structure of the brain... [Thus] The left hemisphere is ultimately dependent on, one might say parasitical on, the right, though it seems to have no awareness of this fact.
>
> *(Ibid.: 5–6)*

This remarkable brain structure is not, of course, peculiar to human beings. It is widespread among vertebrates, from rats to birds, and it seems to be adapted to serve their need to attend to the world in two quite distinct ways. As McGilchrist says:

> there is a need to focus attention narrowly and with precision, as a bird, for example, needs to focus on a grain of corn... At the same time there is a need for open attention, as wide as possible, to guard against a possible predator. Not only are these two different exercises that need to be carried on simultaneously, they are two different *kinds* of exercise, requiring, not just that attention should be divided but that it should be of two different types at once.
>
> *(Ibid.: 25, original emphasis)*

We can often see birds alternating their attitudes in this way, but we know that they need to have both approaches available all the time. Thus the strange and apparently clumsy duplication of faculties that we find makes good sense at an entirely practical level. In order to survive at all, creatures have to combine two quite distinct attitudes to the world and they have to have both of them ready for the occasions when they may be needed.

ONE PERSON OR TWO?

When these strange facts about the way the brain works were first discovered people began to ask the puzzling question: how many distinct beings are really involved here? The controversy chiefly centred on the case of "split-brain patients", people who had the connection between their hemispheres severed for medical purposes, but of course what this procedure reveals about the structure of their brains must also be true of the rest of us.

Are there, then, at least in the case of humans, actually two separate people here, two whole personalities present, or is there only one? R. W. Sperry, who had been responsible for much of this work, was inclined to think that there were indeed two; other people insisted that there could only be one. Nagel, however, rejects both of these views. There is, he said, no whole number of individual minds present, neither one nor two. What, after all would those figures mean? What, really, is a single person?

> We take ourselves as paradigms of psychological unity and are then unable to project ourselves into [these people's] mental lives, either once or twice... We are subtly ignoring the possibility that *our own unity may be nothing absolute,* but merely another case of integration, more or less effective, in the control system of a complex organism.
>
> The unity of our own consciousness may be less clear than we had supposed. The natural conception of a single person controlled by a mind possessing a single visual field... may come into conflict with the physiological facts when it is applied to ourselves.
>
> *(Ibid.: 163, 164, emphasis added)*

Well, so it may, but what is surprising about that? Long before we ever heard about these hemispheres this natural conception of unity had already come into conflict within us with the psychological facts: with facts so striking that we hit our heads against them almost every day. We know well that we are divided beings, full of conflicts that are continually shaping our lives. Attempts at "integration, more or less effective" are our normal business. They are what happens all the time inside the "self" of which people now offer to deprive us and it is hard to see how our lives could go on for a minute without attention to these activities.

Plays and novels exist because this inner strife continually insists on being reported. We know that our individual unity is not a state fully attained but an enterprise, an effort, an aspiration that is central to our lives, all the more central because we are so much troubled by the clashes.

What sort of unity, then, can we actually aspire to? A friend of mine who was much bothered by these things used to compare it to the unity of a committee: a body that has real difficulty in reaching agreement but which knows very well that it has to do so in the long run. In this committee, he said, sometimes the wrong person speaks up and things go very badly. But all the same the committee cannot dissolve itself. There is no real alternative to agreement because, in spite of these difficulties, these parts do compose a single organism. The conflicts that trouble it are internal clashes within this whole person: clashes between motives, between ideals, between visions, between loyalties, between conflicting views of life.

Nagel concludes that our impression of unity is an illusion. I do not think it is any more of an illusion than the impression of duality; there is some truth in both these ideas but the situation is complex. He writes, "it is possible that the ordinary, simple idea of a single person will come to seem quaint one day, when the complexities of the human control system become clearer and we become less certain that there is anything very important that we are *one* of" (*ibid*;: 164, original emphasis). But this is nothing new. We know already that that idea of a single person is far from simple, as our puzzles about responsibility show. It seems to me that the changes we most need are more likely to come from understanding our own lives better, mainly through the existing direct channels – through self-knowledge – than from neuroscience, even though in this context neuroscience is indeed very illuminating.

We are well aware that we are not separate sealed units. As Charles Eisenstein puts it:

> DNA aside, we are all of course permeable to our environment as we routinely exchange materials with the world. We are semi-permanent patterns of flux with an existence independent of the specific material substances that compose us, just as an ocean wave only temporarily comprises a certain collection of water molecules. The molecules simply bob up and down as the wave moves forward onto new ones. Similarly, even though the matter of the universe cycles through each of us at varying rates and in a unique way, we share this matter and, in our relationships, co-determine each other's ever-mutating patterns of flux. Neither the matter nor its patterning constitute autonomous, independent units. The self has only a conditional reality.
>
> *(Eisenstein 2007: 57)*

What it is conditional on – what it depends on – is our own choice: our wish and determination to unify, to make sense of all this shifting water. And what makes this process so difficult now is the cultural shift that has led us to drift away from doing what was traditionally known as psychology – from seriously studying the facts of motivation and devising conceptual maps to explain them – and instead to attempt to study the mind indirectly by more "scientific" means, that is, by something that looks more like chemistry or physics.

That was the spirit in which, in the 1960s, scientifically minded people dismissed Freud and Marx, who both have serious and useful ideas on these topics, to the status of pseudoscientists because they used methods that directly suited their subject matter, rather than ones copied from physical sciences. In spite of this, however, Freud's notion of the ego, super-ego and id has proved so useful that, despite his demotion, we still often use it, and we could certainly do so more effectively if it had been properly developed as it should have been. Similarly Jung, who made really helpful suggestions about deep psychological problems, appears now scarcely to be on the syllabus at all, while Nietzsche has been safely cordoned off somewhere in the humanities.

The core of the trouble here, however, is, of course, not that we don't study the appropriate sages but that we have been deliberately deterred – indeed, actively warned off – from directly attending to ourselves and to those around us at all. The bizarre anti-self campaign which is the main subject of this book is surely intended, among other things, to put us off taking notice of everybody's inner life: to persuade us that this is a trivial, contemptible subject by the simple device of pretending that it isn't there.

12

THE SUPERNATURAL ASPECTS OF PHYSICS

We have now examined various ways in which it is natural for us to think of the self as something divided. We have seen how these approaches all tell us some important truths, how they explain why we do indeed have various divisions within us. But we must surely end up by concluding that, even in the fascinating case of the two brain hemispheres, a human being is still, for central purposes, more one thing than two.

How, then, has our tradition managed to drift so deep into dualist thinking? How, in particular, have we become so committed to this specially awkward kind of dualism in which we now seem to risk losing an invaluable half?

As we have seen, this story is complicated, reaching back to the seventeenth century and beyond. But there is one important aspect of it that we have not yet examined fully, an aspect

DOI: 10.4324/9781003411710-13

which, as we have seen, is actually older still, going back to Plato and Pythagoras. This is the special metaphysical kind of reverence for physics and for the human faculties that engage in physics: a reverence which suggests that this is the only direct window on reality.

Here again Einstein gives us a helpful example. In a letter to the widow of a fellow physicist who had just died he wrote this remarkable sentence, "People like us, who believe in physics, know that the distinction between past, present and future is only a stubbornly persistent illusion". This remark has two quite separate meanings. The obvious one is the familiar observation that spiritual realities are timeless: that the value of a friendship is not lost merely because one of the friends has died. But the other meaning, which comes home only to people familiar with the subject, is that current physics is itself timeless: that, like mathematics, it abstracts from change and depicts the world as change-free.

Modern physical theories, which first arose from enquiries about phenomena where time is irrelevant, such as the rotation of planets, still concentrate on such reversible processes and do not readily accommodate real, irreversible change. Indeed, in the seventeenth century, when nobody had heard of the Big Bang, these cosmic patterns were themselves believed to be unchanging and eternal. This gives a very different background from the evolutionary one that rules today, where we take continuous development for granted.

Ray Monk explains this remarkable fact in his review of Lee Smolin's book *Time Reborn: From the Crisis of Physics to the Future of the Universe*:

> That the passing of time is an illusion is now the orthodoxy among theoretical physicists... The reason physicists have come to reject the reality of time is that they have been

bewitched by the beauty and success of the mathematical models they use into mistaking those models for reality... If we can have timeless truths in mathematics, why not in physics?

(Monk 2013: 8)

Smolin, it seems, is exceptional in that he flatly refuses to accept this attitude, however prevalent it may be, because he thinks (surely rightly) that its arises from philosophical assumptions rather than from scientific argument. He writes:

Nothing we know or experience gets closer to the heart of nature than the reality of time...

The objects of mathematics – curves, numbers etc – do not exist, whereas physics concerns itself with what does exist, and in reality, in the domain of things that do exist, time is inescapable... "Useful as mathematics has turned out to be, the postulation of timeless mathematical laws is never completely innocent, for it always carries a trace of the metaphysical fantasy of transcendence from our earthly world."

(Ibid., quoting Smolin 2013: xii, 14)

In short, *time needs to be classed as an illusion only if we decide to define reality as shaped by the current ideas of physicists*, rather than – as most of past and present humanity would naturally think – by what is an unremovable part of the world that we all have to deal with, as time unmistakeably is. And since today's physics is always on the move and is full of unresolved conflicts, the idea of making our concept of reality depend on it is not seductive.

Physicists themselves are not (it seems) now quite unanimous on the point of time's unreality, as appears from a survey in *New Scientist* under the title "Space Versus Time; One Has to Go", asking for a new theory of space-time (Ananthaswamy 2013). But mostly they take sides against time, a decision that (as I have suggested) surely reflects a choice of abstractions for conceptual convenience rather than any newly established fact about the world. What they are really saying is not "we now know that time does not exist" – which, being a sentence in the present tense, would probably be self-contradictory – but simply "time is not relevant to our calculations". In short, time is no business of physicists. But then plenty of other things, from frogs to parliaments, are not their business either, and that does not stop them being real.

Smolin suggests that this rejection of time arises from a conviction that the imagined, changeless, abstract, transcendent universe that physicists prefer to study is somehow more real than the changeable concrete one that is familiar to us, even though we don't actually live in it. But what does this contention mean? An interesting point that arises here is: why pick on time and space? Nobody seems to be saying that heat (for instance) is an illusion, although, of course, it too has its own scientific description. Scientifically speaking, heat is, it seems, just the kinetic energy of motion of atoms. But when people say that they feel hot or mention heat in discussions of climate change this aspect does not need to be mentioned because it is not relevant. Ordinary uses of the term are well understood without bringing accusations of illusion. Should not the same thing be true of time?

Whatever may be thought of this debate among physicists, however, Einstein's meaning is surely clear. For him the spiritual proposition about the lasting value of friendship comes as an integral part of physics, something not available to outsiders. It is something that "people like us who believe in physics" know and other people don't.

It is at this point that the two possible meanings that I noted at the outset for Crick's oracular pronouncement begin to appear, not as separate options but, rather sinisterly, as two sides of the same coin. For if reality was indeed something that only physicists could reach – if everybody else was wandering clueless through a hopeless maze of illusions – then there would be a crucial difference between these scientists and the rest of us. We are being told that we are mere peasants, helpless "folk-psychologists", and we may well hear this dictum as a simple insult: "you are nothing".

This is the story that makes science strike non-scientists as an alien and intrusive dictator. It has, however, no real basis. The entities in which physics deals – quarks, electrons, black holes and so forth – are no more real than any individual's own joys and sorrows, fears and ambitions, or indeed than the road he is just going to cross. They are just exceptionally abstract entities, forming parts of theories that are exceptionally general.

There is no rivalry, no competition, between these different kinds of item for the status of reality. They are all real because they are all aspects of the one world in which we live. These abstractions do, of course, have a special sort of importance in our thought when we are asking very general questions about the physical world. They make it possible to theorize about that world on an impressively vast scale. But the theories that are formed in this way are still parts of human thought. They gain their importance from their relation to the rest of life. They are not a window into a quite different spiritual world, a divine realm of numbers that contains the ultimate explanation of everything here.

MIND THE GAP!

If all this is true – if current materialism has all these drawbacks – the next question must surely be: how has so odd a theory come to be so widely accepted? As we have seen, the answer is simple; this is simply the last stage in the collapse of dualism.

From the seventeenth to the nineteenth centuries, most scientists believed implicitly in a separate soul and body. This conviction was largely backed by Christian doctrine, and, although it was always hard to see how the two might interact, people could regard them as roughly equally necessary. Matter was assumed to be inert and lifeless: mere passive stuff to be moved by spirit, that is, ultimately by God. Great trouble was taken to avoid attributing to it any independent power and especially to avoid positing a beneficent Mother Nature so as not to infringe God's monopoly as Creator. As we have seen, the men of the Royal Society were strong advocates of this exclusive, dramatic, patriarchal form of dualism, and they objected particularly to Nature because she was apparently female.

There were, of course, always people who tried to resolve the awkward dualist world picture by proving that chalk was really cheese or vice versa. Some, like Thomas Hobbes, tried to do it by reducing mind to inert matter. Others preferred to reduce matter to mind, like Hume, who, though resistant to religion, thought everything was basically composed of disconnected atoms of perception. As lately as the start of the twentieth century, people like Bertrand Russell and William James saw this choice between idealistic and materialistic reduction as still an open option. But then there occurred one of those strange cultural earthquakes that overturn the tables, making what is familiar suddenly appear unthinkable. Idealism went right out of fashion.

The balance had, of course, been gradually shifting in this direction throughout the nineteenth century and the scenery was becoming very different. On the one hand, physical science had made enormous strides; on the other, the churches were losing their authority. Politically, powerful religious bodies had backed objectionable governments, so they were now widely seen as oppressors. The revolutionary temper of the times seemed simply to call for religion as such to be abolished, and it seemed natural to suppose that the soul should go along with it. Thus the mind–body gap would be closed by dropping one terminus: the mind.

WHY THE DIVISION?

At this point it was really necessary to stand back from the traditional mind–body problem and look afresh at the whole situation. Why were we divided into these two parts in the first place? Why was the conflict between Science and Religion – which were seen as the social representatives of these two forces – thought to be so important? These are, after all, only two among many aspects of that very complex thing, human life. The relation between them can really only be grasped by finding where they stand in that wider pattern.

Dualism itself and both the twin reductions that stem from it are all answers to a single question, namely: *what stuff is everything made of?* Nagel suggests that we should answer this question by some kind of "neutral monism", that is, by supposing that some third stuff, neither mind nor matter, is present to underlie both of them (Nagel 2012: 37). Russell used sometimes to recommend this, but it seems to me that we should do much better by ceasing to ask that particular question. Searching for an underlying stuff is a useful plan when we are talking about physical objects but it is not at all obviously appropriate when we are talking about things of different kinds, such as cheese and thought.

Physically, we have now discovered a good deal about what stuff human beings are made of. We have done this by taking them to pieces – of course, always in socially acceptable ways. *But there is no parallel method by which we can take their thoughts to pieces,* even though many seekers after a scientific psychology wanted

to do this in the nineteenth century. Thought just has no ultimate units. It is not granular; it is continuous.

This means that we have to find a different imagery. We cannot understand the function of our inner life by trying to find
the stuff that it is made of because nobody made it and it isn't
made of anything. What we have to do instead is find out its
relation to a wider whole: to the whole person in the first place
and then to the wider community.

Might it be more realistic if, instead of positing two separate
stuffs, we used here the image of exploring a vast landscape, a
landscape that can be approached from various angles but can't
be laid open from a single point? This image does get some
things right. The trouble with it is that it suggests that, if we
want to bring the viewpoints together, we need only cut down
some trees, that is, we can reduce one viewpoint to the other
by abstraction. Another image that proves attractive here is that
of operating on "different levels". This can be helpful, but it too
has a built-in weakness in that the "lower level" may easily be
thought of as grander – more real, more fundamental – than
those above it. And this again would mean that everything really boils down to physics. That sense of hierarchy very easily
affects all these gravitational metaphors, from Descartes' picture of foundations to the present day.

I think a better image may come from a rather closer com-
parison: from the case, which I have already mentioned, of
the relation between sight and touch. Here there is no possibility of reducing one kind of perception to the other or of
claiming that one is more real than the other. The table that
you see and handle is one table, not two joined together. You
have two perceptions of it, both incomplete, and you have to
do what you can to being them together. A similar relation is
also seen in rather more dramatic form in the case of lightning
and thunder.

So, to return to the case of inner and outer vision, if you are trying to understand unhappiness, either your own or someone else's, you can proceed either physically from the outside, by observation and medical means, or psychologically, by sympathy and imagination. But there is nothing to stop you doing both. And, since we are such complex beings, the twofold approach is surely to be strongly recommended. The alternative system, where specialists in these two approaches settle their difference by tribal warfare, does not seem to work so well.

ATTENDING TO MATTER

Altogether, then, the dualist picture needed a good deal of rethinking. Rather than take this trouble, however, our intellectual ancestors preferred to accept the separate mind and body as given units, to treat them as warring rivals and then simply to take sides in their conflict. Those who wanted to ditch religion were then naturally drawn to the idea of closing the gap by dropping Mind altogether and espousing materialism as a creed instead. In fact, they decided to believe only in Matter.

But this cannot work, not if we also want to believe in evolution. Matter, as dualists conceived it, is far too inert a stuff to have produced the whole living world that we see. In order for all this life to have evolved, the basic stuff of the world has to have been something capable of activity, something creative enough to generate these varied forms. Natural selection, which is supposed to explain evolution, does not, of course, explain this richness; it only explains why some of these forms have prevailed over others. And it has nothing at all to say about the origin of life. Of course, today's physicists do indeed think of this basic stuff as active. They no longer speak of it in terms of solid, inert particles but of fields, forces and energy: words that describe their interrelation rather than their nature.

All this means that the original dualist division into mind and body had hopeless drawbacks and certainly should not be used for further development. As we have noticed, dualism does not mention the intermediate term *life*, leaving it undescribable in either physical or spiritual terms. And this failure has persisted, resulting, for instance, in the fact that the standard dictionary of biology simply has no entry for this rather crucial term.

This life-blindness is important because it quite obscures the continuity of evolution. It is surely more natural to suppose that the world developed gradually and coherently, without a break, from rocks through rabbits to Einstein and beyond, than to divide it arbitrarily into these two irreconcilable provinces. As Aristotle remarked, "Nature proceeds little by little from things lifeless to animal life in such a way that it is impossible to determine the exact line of demarcation" (*History of Animals*, viii, 1), a reflection that still makes sense today as evolutionists bicker about the various precursors of life.

Another frontier at which the dualist approach shows its absurdity is the borderline of mind. Here philosophers agonize ceaselessly about what they call the "hard problem" of consciousness: namely, how can thought and feeling possibly occur in a world that is made up only of dead, inert matter? Well, if it really was such a world they doubtless couldn't. And this is one more reason – if another was needed on top of the whole story of evolution as we now have it - for not assuming that matter is thus inert and dead.

IS MIND, THEN, A BY-PRODUCT?

So, one way or another, the policy of splitting everything into mind and matter turned out badly. Once that division was made, however, people were bound to try to deal with it by dropping one of the two terms. And that device was bound to make things worse.

During the eighteenth and nineteenth centuries, scientists gradually dropped the idea of mind. They came increasingly to regard materialism as their fallback creed. They did not notice the serious difficulties that we have been considering because these lay far from the lit-up areas of the day. What did catch their attention, however, was another difficulty. What were they to do with the thoughts and feelings that still unquestionably kept occurring to them?

In the 1880s, T. H. Huxley suggested his steam-whistle solution to this problem, now more elegantly known as "epiphenomenalism", a solution that, for the lack of a better story, is still in use today. Huxley proposed that our thoughts and feelings are simply idle side effects of our actions. Like the whistle that an engine lets off when it starts moving, they are picturesque and striking, but they don't drive the train. Thus we are "conscious automata".

Huxley himself does not seem to have attached any special importance to this idea. It was one of many that he constantly threw off, like sparks from a Roman candle, much as Haldane later did, leaving other people to make what they could of them. The materialists of his day, however, eagerly seized this suggestion as a way of getting mental activity out of the way. They firmly ignored the fact that motives and plans can't be side effects because they always occur *before* an action rather than after it, and also that (as we noticed in Einstein's case) problems don't solve themselves without some conscious attention. Thus, with the same devout docility that they attribute to medieval schoolmen, scientists agreed to preserve their materialist creed by signing up for a tale that, as anyone can see, does not actually make sense at all.

During the nineteenth and twentieth centuries, various trends converged to encourage this policy. Confidence in the machine model, which had been growing ever since Descartes launched it, was boosted by technological successes from steam engines to the moonshots. Mechanistic thinking made it seem increasingly plausible that everything, including humans, was really a machine. It was conveniently forgotten that *real machines actually need real minds to design them.*

When we talk of any living thing (including a human) as a machine we are using a metaphor. Living things aren't machines; no one made them; they are here because they have grown. But from the moment when Descartes was first stage-struck by those startling clockwork automata, observers discussing these things have found it impossible to remember this difference. Thus even John Searle, who is usually a beacon of sanity among a distraction of fogs and phantoms, wrote the following bit of dialogue in his discussion of "machine intelligence":

"Could a machine think?"
The answer is obviously, yes. We are precisely such machines.
(Searle 1981: 368)

He goes on, of course, to argue that there is therefore no reason to suppose that real, literal machines are seriously different. But the whole argument is hollow. We are not such machines. Nobody designed us. We are animals. We are as we are because we have grown that way.

This unthinking use of the machine metaphor is interesting because, in theory, the members of the Royal Society strongly disapproved of all metaphors, requiring instead that enlightened scientists should describe their facts directly in plain language. Locke was particularly stern about such "vague and insignificant forms of speech" (Locke [1689] 1997: "Epistle to the Reader", 11). But using machine imagery has now become so habitual in these contexts that people evidently no longer know when they are doing it.

Besides this influence from machines, belief in evolution provided a plausible story about how matter could have formed the world without spiritual help. And, beyond this, scientists came increasingly to feel that rationality required a single pattern of thought that should rule everywhere: in some sense a Theory of Everything, which must not be distorted to fit in the varying viewpoints of separate subjects. The virtue of objectivity seemed, therefore, to demand a world composed entirely of objects. Subjects would have to be abolished.

All these and other similar trends took things in the same direction, but the development that finally launched this anti-subject campaign was probably the invention of modern brain-imaging methods, especially functional resonance magnetic imaging (fRMI). This provided simple graphic pictures of the alleged machine that could now be seen as taking over all distinctively human functions: the brain. It led to the hope that this was the only thing that needed to be studied.

Just as the behaviourists had concluded – after ruling that everything else was unscientific – that human life could be fully understood by simply observing the physical details of behaviour, so today's reductivists have decided that it can henceforward all be safely left to neurological experiments. This would, of course, be the ultimate trouble-saver for psychology; if it worked, everybody else could now go home. And it is perhaps rather sad that (as has been mentioned before) both these schemes are just promissory materialism: visionary drafts on an imaginary future that have no kind of prospect of being redeemed.

Instead, enquiries about this vast subject will have to go on, as they have done so far, through an endless series of enterprises that are set up to solve particular questions, enterprises that gradually accumulate some measure of good sense but need to be lit up constantly by the fire of serious attention to actual life. There is no short cut.

CONCLUSION
ON BEING STILL HERE

In this book we have been tracing the history of what is surely a strange development. We have been asking how it has come about that a number of highly educated and sophisticated scholars – people dedicated to the life of the mind – are now claiming that their own minds, and other people's minds too, do not exist.

As we have seen, this mechanistic materialism has become an orthodoxy today, professed by scientists and many other people in the half-casual way in which people used formerly to recite the Christian creeds, without any notion of making it the basis of their lives. We have seen that they seldom actually try to live by it. In fact, it would be quite impossible for any human to live their life on that basis, most obviously because of its consequences for free will, but the basic logic of the whole situation is also fatal to it. So why is this happening?

DOI: 10.4324/9781003411710-14

Hoping to understand it, we have looked at a long history of earlier thought that does go some way to explain it. We have seen how previously favoured ideas – not only behaviourist ones but much older traditions as well – have not died but have twisted themselves round in a way that made this kind of exclusive materialism seem natural. We have seen in several cases how myths – imaginative visions, dramas attached to certain beliefs – persist and deeply influence people even after the beliefs themselves have officially died. But we are still left with something strange: with people who profess a doctrine that seems to contradict the obvious facts and who sometimes seem to revel in this paradox. How does this come about?

Unkind critics have suggested that it happens because the belief in question is only supposed to apply to *other people* – patients, clients and experimental subjects – and not to the speakers themselves. I think there is much in this. Psychologists do sometimes theorize in this way, and the behaviourists in particular often did so. And it is interesting that Crick initially makes his claim in the second person. He doesn't say "I have just realised that I am an illusion". It is *you*, not himself, that he at once consigns to the bin.

He and his colleagues do indeed officially cover their own cases as well. But the problems of that aspect don't seem to interest them much. So it is possible that this self-exceptionalism may partly explain this line of theorizing. But in order to attract so many distinguished academic minds something rather deeper than this has surely been at work.

I think the hidden ingredient is something that I mentioned in the first pages of this book: the idea that scientific doctrine is not meant to apply to the vulgar, common-sense world that we ordinary humans live in. Instead, it is intended to describe a separate, more refined, possibly Platonic world that only scientists can perceive. Wolpert usefully expressed this thought in his book *The Unnatural Nature of Science* (1992) when he wrote that nobody should be surprised when science clashes with common sense because there is no relation between these two systems. Physics, which is the only true science is, he said, unique: a wholly independent enterprise cut off from all the rest of human thought. It embodies an ideal at which all other thought should aim, but which it can never attain:

> In a sense, all science aspires to be like physics, and physics aspires to be like mathematics... In spite of recent successes, biology has a long way to go when measured against physics or chemistry. What hope is there for sociology acquiring a physics-like lustre?...
>
> By ignoring the achievements of science, by ignoring whether a theory is right or wrong, by denying progress, the sociologists have missed the core of the scientific enterprise... I must side with Francis Bacon, who, 400 years ago, urged that those interested in science ought to "throw aside all thought of philosophy or at least expect but little and poor fruit from it".
>
> *(Wolpert 1992: 121–2)*

Thus, in the view of these devotees, physics alone can break out of the human limitations that imprison all the rest of our thinking. It alone enables us to confront reality directly. Just as Plato believed that the soul – when suitably trained – can directly perceive the virtues, so (these people tell us) the scientifically trained intellect can directly perceive physical reality, untrammelled by the confusing effects of human senses and customs.

This ambition to transcend humanity is rather touching and (as we have seen) it is certainly not new, but it is, nonetheless, unfortunately doomed. For, clearly, physics draws all its data from human sense-perception, just as the other sciences do. Its thinking starts from the ordinary data of sense and proceeds through categories formed by human experience until it is finally carried through by human minds. Just like the other sciences, physics does not make progress by getting rid of ordinary human thought but by using it in order to correct particular human errors – gradually and painfully – so as finally to get nearer to certain humanly accessible aspects of the truth.

Nothing superhuman is needed here. The faculties by which all the sciences work are human faculties, continuous with the ones we use in everyday life. This continuity is plain when we notice how prevalent, and how important, metaphors drawn from ordinary experience have always been in science. New thinking always needs to go back to its natural roots. And the aim of the whole effort is not to reach an alien world by getting outside the human sphere. It is to make the best sense we can of what human life can show us.

There is no need, therefore, to flatter mathematics and physics by representing them as remote ideals that other subjects should imitate. They are splendid arts in their own right as well as being useful to the other sciences. But those other sciences do not need to cherish any desperate, frustrated longing to become more like them. They all do different work. And they all contribute to a whole that grows from the soil of common sense, to which they are therefore still ultimately answerable.

Plato's suggestion about the virtues made a quite different point. There we do need to use patterns of thinking that are appropriate to understanding questions of value: patterns that are not the ones used for dealing with questions about facts that do not matter to us. These practical patterns are quite closely allied to our emotional nature. We use them when we are puzzled, as we often are, to see how to act – to see which of the courses before us is the more important or the more serious – to see which of them we ought to attend to. These questions about value are of quite a different kind from any that could arise in physics.

Wolpert's declaration is a prime case of scientism, the deliberate, arbitrary isolation of something called Science (essentially physics) from the rest of thought. As we have seen, this isolation has been shaped by various powerful earlier belief systems, notably by dualism in general and the Platonic or Pythagorean forms of it in particular. It keeps the shape that they impressed on it, even though the people who profess it now don't know this and explain it quite differently.

Why does this one kind of thought have this special status? Wolpert writes as if all other organized human thinking – all the arts and crafts, history, poetry, geography, musicology, linguistics, logic and the rest of it – did not exist. These disciplined ways of thinking are, however, what has enabled the human race to deal with the fearful range of problems that has confronted it during countless aeons, problems quite unlike the highly abstract ones that are railed off for physics and certainly no less important.

As we have seen, it is out of this immense general striving of thought that the modern sciences and the other academic disciplines have grown. They are subcultures that have emerged within this vast general effort to understand the world. Each of them deals with its own range of problems, and each often needs to develop specialized ways of thinking. This specialization is not, as Wolpert suggests, a distinctive mark of physical science. (Perhaps he should try a problem in history – for instance, interpreting an ancient inscription in an unknown script – and see how much physics helps him there.) But in developing these technical methods they don't part company with the basic understanding of life that forms part of the human inheritance. They use it as the foundation for everything else that they build.

I have suggested that we might see these newer, more specialized ways of thinking, acting and talking as being like forms of vegetation that grow on the surface of life and are liable to change. The soil and rock below do not alter. Life is essentially the same for us now as it was for our remotest ancestors. And although common sense always incorporates some of the surface vegetation for everyday purposes, it is always deeply grounded in the earth below. The new skills are left-brain business. If we are to fit them into the rest of life we need to use our entire brains, with both halves working together.

If we then ask whether awareness of the inner life – of private, personal thoughts, feelings, impressions and dreams – belongs to the soil or to the current crop, all experience tells us that it belongs to the soil. In spite of the huge differences between cultures, all that we know about human behaviour shows that it can be understood only by reference to people's own thoughts, dreams, hopes, fears and other feelings. This is not something invented by a particular culture. It is universal. And when we try to understand the immediate behaviour of those around us we absolutely need our familiar map of the possible moods and motives that might shape their actions. Above all, we need an understanding of the possible conflicts among them.

The idea that reports of brain movements could ever replace this direct understanding is surely a fantasy. It seems to be a prime case of left-hemisphere-biased error, tunnel vision that grows from an overconcentration on a particular range of details. In Chapter 11 I likened it to the attitude of an obsessive archaeologist who can't stop digging to see what is happening on the rest of the site. But since these metaphysicians apparently own a private line to reality, it may be better to compare them, more grandly, to Pythagorean mystics, so busy contemplating the heavenly multiverse that they don't notice they are living in climate change. Either way, they surely need to come back to life on the ordinary surface of this earth along with the rest of us:

Does the fish soar to find the ocean,
    The eagle plunge to seek the air –
That we ask of the stars in motion
    If they have rumour of thee there?

Not where the wheeling systems darken
    And our benumbed conceiving soars! –
The drift of pinions, would we hearken,
    Beats at our own clay–shuttered doors.

(Francis Thompson, The Kingdom of God*)*

BIBLIOGRAPHY

Ananthaswamy, A. 2013. "Space vs Time: One Has to Go". *New Scientist* 2921 (15 June): 34–7.

Ananthaswamy, A. & G. Lawton 2013. "When the Self Breaks". *New Scientist* 2905 (23 February): 36–42.

Barkham, P. 2010. "My Search for the Purple Emperor Butterfly". *Guardian G2* (5 October): 6.

Barrow, J. & F. Tipler 1986. *The Anthropic Cosmological Principle*. Oxford: Oxford University Press.

Blakemore, C. 1999. *The Mind Machine*. London: BBC Books.

Bond, M. 2013. "The Living Heart of Things". *New Scientist* 2931 (24 August): 48.

Boyle, R. 1722. *The Works of the Honourable Robert Boyle*, vol. 5, T. Birch (ed.). London.

Carpenter, R. 2013. "Widen the Search". *New Scientist* 2941 (2 November): 32.

Chesterton, G. K. 1940. "The Blue Cross". In *The Innocence of Father Brown*. Quoted in S. Conway Morris, *Life's Solution: Inevitable Humans in a Lonely Universe* (Cambridge: Cambridge University Press, 2003).

Conway Morris, S. 2003. *Life's Solution: Inevitable Humans in a Lonely Universe*. Cambridge: Cambridge University Press.

Crick, F. 1994. *The Astonishing Hypothesis: The Scientific Search For The Soul*. New York: Touchstone.

Cronin, H. 1991. *The Ant and the Peacock: Sexual Selection from Darwin to Today*. Cambridge: Cambridge University Press.

Darwin, C. [1871] 1981. *The Descent of Man and Selection in Relation to Sex*. Princeton, NJ: Princeton University Press.

Darwin, C. 1872. *The Expression of the Emotions in Man and Animals*. London: John Murray.

Darwin, C. & T. H. Huxley 1974. *Autobiographies*. Oxford: Oxford University Press.

Davies, P 2006. *The Goldilocks Enigma: Why is the Universe Just Right for Life?* London: Allen Lane.

Dawkins, R. 1995. *River Out Of Eden: A Darwinian View of Life*. London: Phoenix.

Eisenstein, C. 2007. *The Ascent of Humanity: The Age of Separation, the Age of Reunion, and the Convergence of Crises that is Birthing the Transition*. Harrisburg, PA: Panenthea Press.

Eldredge, N. 2004. *Why We Do It: Rethinking Sex and the Selfish Gene*. New York: Norton.

Farringdon, B. 1970. *The Philosophy of Francis Bacon*. Liverpool: Liverpool University Press.

Ficino, M. 1956. *Commentaire sur le Banquet de Platon*, R. Marcel (trans.). Paris: Les Belles Lettres.

Fisher, R. 2013. "The End?" *New Scientist* 2905 (23 February): 43.

Gazzaniga, M. 2008. *Human: The Science Behind What Makes Us Unique*. London: HarperCollins.

Glanvill, J. 1970. *The Vanity of Dogmatising: The Three Visions*, S. Medcalf (ed.), 1661 version. Brighton: Harvester.

Goodwin, B. 1994. *How the Leopard Changed its Spots*. London: Phoenix.

Greenfield, S. 2000. *Brain Story: Unlocking Our Inner World of Emotions, Memories, Ideas and Desires*. London: BBC Books.

Greenfield, S. 2008. *ID: The Quest for Identity in the Twenty–first Century*. London: Sceptre.

Holmes, B. 2013a. "Earth After Life". *New Scientist* 2936 (28 September): 39.

Holmes, B. 2013b. "Life's Purpose: Might Organisms Have Some Power to Direct Their Own Evolution?" *New Scientist* 2938 (12 October): 33.

Locke, J. [1689] 1997. *An Essay Concerning Human Understanding*, R. Woolhouse (ed.). London: Penguin.

Low, P., D. Edelman & C. Koch 2012. "The Cambridge Declaration On Consciousness". Proclaimed at the Francis Crick Memorial Conference on Consciousness in Human and non–Human Animals at

Churchill College, Cambridge. http://fcmconference.org/img/CambridgeDeclarationOnConsciousness.pdf (accessed December 2013).

Margulis, L. 1995. *What is Life?* London: Weidenfeld & Nicolson.

McGilchrist, I. 2009. *The Master and his Emissary: The Divided Brain and the Making of the Modern World.* New Haven, CT: Yale University Press.

Midgley, M. 2003. *The Myths We Live By.* London: Routledge.

Miller, G. 2001. *The Mating Mind: How Sexual Choice Shaped the Evolution of Human Nature.* London: Vintage.

Monk, R. 2013. Review of Lee Smolin, *Time Reborn: From The Crisis of Physics to the Future of the Universe. Guardian* (8 June): 8. www.theguardian.com/books/2013/jun/06/time-reborn-lee-smolin-review (accessed December 2013).

Nagel, T. 1979. *Mortal Questions.* Cambridge: Cambridge University Press.

Nagel, T. 1985. *The View From Nowhere.* Oxford: Oxford University Press.

Nagel, T. 1994. "Consciousness and Objective Reality". In *The Mind–Body Problem: A Guide to the Current Debate,* R. Warner & T. Szubka (eds), 63–8. Oxford: Blackwell.

Nagel, T. 2012. *Mind and Cosmos: Why the Materialist Neo–Darwinist Conception of Nature is Almost Certainly False.* Oxford: Oxford University Press.

New Scientist 2013. "Who Are You?" *New Scientist* 2905 (23 February): 32–43.

Nowak, M. A., C. E. Tarnita & E. O. Wilson 2010. "The Evolution of Eusociality". *Nature* 466 (26 August): 1057–62.

Regan, T. & P. Singer 1986. *Animal Rights and Human Obligations.* Englewood Cliffs, NJ: Prentice Hall.

Robinson, M. 2010. *Absence of Mind: The Dispelling of Inwardness from the Modern Myth of the Self.* New Haven, CT: Yale University Press.

Searle, J. 1981. "Minds, Brains and Programs". In *The Mind's I,* D. R. Hofstadter & D. Dennett (eds), 353–72. Brighton: Harvester Press.

Sloan Wilson, D. 2008. "Why Richard Dawkins Is Wrong About Religion". In *The Edge Of Reason,* A. Bentley (ed.). London: Continuum.

Sloan Wilson, D. 2010. "Super–evolution: Change for the Common Good", *New Scientist* 2781 (9 October): 34.

Smolin, L. 2013. *Time Reborn: From the Crisis in Physics to the Future of the Universe.* London: Allen Lane.

Sperry, R. W. 1964. "The Great Cerebral Commissure". *Scientific American* 210: 42.

Strawson, G. 2008. "Realistic Monism: Why Physicalism Entails Panpsychism". In his *Real Materialism and Other Essays,* 53–74. Oxford: Clarendon Press.

Strawson, G. 2013. "Real Naturalism". *London Review of Books* 35(18) (26 September): 28–30.

Tallis, R. 2011. *Aping Mankind: Neuromania, Darwinitis and the Misrepresentation of Humanity*. Durham: Acumen.

Vrecko, S. 2010. "Neuroscience, Power and Culture: An Introduction". In *History of the Human Sciences* 23(1): 1–10.

Warnock, G. 1967. *Contemporary Moral Philosophy*. London: Macmillan.

Weinberg, S. 1977. *The First Three Minutes*. London: Deutsch.

Wertheim, M. 1997. *Pythagoras' Trousers: God, Physics and the Gender Wars*. London: Fourth Estate.

Westerhoff, J. 2013a. "What Are You?" *New Scientist* 2905 (23 February): 34–7.

Westerhoff, J. 2013b. "When Are You?" *New Scientist* 2905 (23 February): 37.

Wilson, E. O. 1975. *Sociobiology: The New Synthesis*. Cambridge, MA: Harvard University Press.

Wittgenstein, L. 1951. *Philosophical Investigations*. Oxford: Blackwell.

Wolpert, L. 1992. *The Unnatural Nature of Science*. London: Faber.

INDEX